The Jumbo Book of

DRAMA

Kids Can Press acknowledges the financial support of the Government of Ontario, through the Ontario Media Development Corporation's Ontario Book Initiative; the Ontario Arts Council; the Canada Council for the Arts; and the Government of Canada, through the BPIDP, for our publishing activity.

Published in Canada by
Kids Can Press Ltd.
29 Birch Avenue
Toronto, ON M4V 1E2

Published in the U.S. by
Kids Can Press Ltd.
2250 Military Road
Tonawanda, NY 14150

www.kidscanpress.com

Edited by Linda Biesenthal
Designed by Julia Naimska
Cover photography by Ray Boudreau
Printed in Hong Kong, China, by WKT Company Limited

This book is limp sewn with drawn-on cover.

CM PA 04 0 9 8 7 6 5 4 3 2 1

National Library of Canada Cataloguing in Publication Data

Dunleavy, Deborah
  The jumbo book of drama / Deborah Dunleavy ; illustrations by Jane Kurisu.

For ages 8 and up.
ISBN 1-55337-008-2

1. Children's plays, Canadian (English). 2. Theater — Study and teaching (Elementary). 3. Drama in education. I. Kurisu, Jane II. Title.

PN1701.D84 2004   372.66'044   C2003-902485-7

Kids Can Press is a Corus™ Entertainment company

To my parents, who always believed in my artistic ways. — D.D.

Acknowledgments

Cheers to the many artists, teachers, mentors and friends who encourage, challenge and defend my artistic pursuits. Thank you all.

Applause to the many children who have taught me what really works in drama. Thanks for the thousands of inspirations. Standing ovation to David Booth, Chuck Lundy, Larry Swartz, Naomi Tyrrell, Karen Waterman, Dan Wood and countless others who have shared their artistic visions over the years.

Bravo to all the drama fans who keep the muse alive through their participation in Ontario's Council of Drama in Education.

To Linda Biesenthal for guiding me on my writing journey. And to Kate for experimenting with my experiments.

The Jumbo Book of
DRAMA

Written by **Deborah Dunleavy**
Illustrated by **Jane Kurisu**

Kids Can Press

Contents

SETTING THE STAGE

Drama takes you into the wonderful world of make believe where anything is possible. You can travel to different times and places and step into someone else's shoes for a while. Explore the jungle or join the circus. Turn yourself into a hero or a villain. Fly by the seat of your pants or battle a fire-breathing dragon.

This book is chock-full of drama activities and ideas to get you started on the stage. Act I takes you on a physical adventure with Mime Magic, Masked Play, Clowning Around and Dance Drama. These four kinds of drama are all about movement — using just your body to tell a story. Act II includes three kinds of drama that will help you find your dramatic voice — Puppets and Puppetry, Readers' Theater and Radio Plays.

In Act III, you get to put body movements and your vocal cords together. Explore characters and plots in Melodrama, Comedy and Tragedy. Act IV takes you behind the scenes where you can learn about sound effects, lighting, costumes, set design and props.

People around the world and all through the ages have used drama to express their beliefs and tell their stories. In these pages, you'll travel back to an amphitheater in ancient Greece, make commedia dell'arte masks from medieval Italy, learn puppetry techniques from Japanese masters, perform an African folktale and an Inuit legend, and talk to King Arthur in your living room.

Here's some advice from one actor to another: Don't be shy! Let your imagination run wild! Have fun! And, as they say in the land of show biz, break a leg!

ACT I: MAKE YOUR MOVE!

In this first act, you'll be doing drama using just your body.
When your voice is silent, you can focus on the way you move.
You'll be amazed at the stories you can tell and all the emotions you
can express with a few twitches and turns of your head, arms,
legs, shoulders, hips and feet. Get ready to explore ...

- Mime Magic
- Masked Play
- Clowning Around
- Dance Drama

MIME MAGIC

Get some friends together and create a world where no words are allowed! Balance on an invisible tightrope. Make a wall appear out of thin air. Juggle an invisible ball. You can do all this without using any words or real objects. Mime needs only your body and your imagination.

- Get trapped in a box.
- Create a white-face.
- Transform yourself into a robot.

The Art of Mime

Mime is the art of silent acting. It's all about using body language and big gestures to express emotions and tell a story.

Mime was first performed in ancient Greece in enormous outdoor theaters with thousands of people watching. Mime actors used huge, exaggerated gestures and movements so that the audience in the back rows could follow the story. Their performances were usually backed up by music or singing.

The Master of Mime

Thanks to Marcel Marceau, the magic of mime is still alive. As a boy in France, Marceau was a natural mimic. In 1946, he began studying the art of mime. A year later, Marceau created Bip — a white-faced clown that became the world's most famous mime character.

The World of Mime

Mime is one of the oldest forms of drama. Mime actors have been entertaining audiences for more than 2000 years. Today, you'll find mimes performing in every corner of the world.

Ancient Rome

The Romans learned the art of mime from the ancient Greeks. In ancient Rome, mimes mostly performed silly comedies on an open stage, sometimes to audiences of more than 50 000 people. The actors wore flour on their faces so the audience could see their expressions.

The Middle Ages

During the Middle Ages, mimes in Italy performed lots of clowning and slapstick. The best-known character in these early Italian comedies (called commedia dell'arte) was an acrobat and dancer named Harlequin.

Getting Started

Like an athlete or a musician, a mime needs to warm up before a performance. Some mimes use freeze-frame exercises to get their body language working. Pretend you're a jogger, and try this warm-up for fun and practice.

Neutral Position

- Stand tall.
- Keep your feet apart — about shoulder width.
- Look straight ahead.

Action

- Start the action suddenly.
- Make all your movements and expressions larger than life.

Freeze Frame

- Suddenly freeze.
- Hold the action.

Neutral Position

- Return to the neutral position.
- Use the neutral position whenever you're starting and ending your mime movements.

More Mime Practice

Try these freeze frames, then make up some of your own. Better yet, get some friends together to pull some freeze-frame ideas out of a hat. See if you can guess what they're doing.

- tightrope walker
- leaping frog
- speed skater

Put on a Face

The expression you put on your face is worth a thousand words. Is your mime character happy, sad, lonely, afraid? Are your eyes open wide in surprise or squinting with suspicion? Play this face-wipe game and practice some mime mugging.

Face-Wipe Game

This game starts with your face in neutral — without any expression.

- Keep your face neutral.
- Place your hands above your head.
- Look straight ahead.

- Hide your face behind your hands — without touching it.
- Put on a sad face.
- Freeze it.

- Lower your hands below your chin.
- Show your sad face.

More Mugging

Try these faces on for size:

- excited
- surprised
- angry
- afraid
- bored
- suspicious

White-Face

Mime makeup, called white-face, creates a neutral face that allows you to show many different feelings. If you have an allergy to makeup, just dust your face with baby powder.

What You Need

- white makeup
- bright red lipstick
- black eyebrow pencil
- baby powder and cotton puffs
- damp facecloth

What You Do

1 Start at your hairline and smooth on the white makeup. Cover your eyebrows and eyelids — but don't cover your eyelashes. Use a damp cloth to wipe off any white-face that gets on your neck or ears.

2 Use a cotton puff to put a bit of baby powder over the white-face.

3 Use your fingernail to trace eyebrows above your own eyebrows. Fill them in with the eyebrow pencil.

4 Keep your eyes open and draw a vertical line above and below each eye. Close your eyes, one at a time, and connect the lines.

6 Fill in the outline with red lipstick.

5 Outline your mouth with the eyebrow pencil. Make your mouth smaller or larger.

7 Use the eyebrow pencil to outline your white-face. Now it looks like a mask.

Ball Games

Baseball, beach ball, goofy ball. Mimes can make all sorts of balls that magically shrink, get heavy or sometimes float away!

Play Ball!

Imagine that there's a magical ball right there — hanging in the air in front of you.

- Reach toward the ball — keep your hands flat!
- Snap your hands into a curved position — you are now holding the ball.

- Feel the weight in one hand, then the other — it's pretty heavy!
- Squeeze the ball into a tiny marble — roll it across the floor.
- Oops! The marble turned into a gigantic balloon! Help! It's floating away!

Juggle a Ball

Hold your ball in one hand and get ready to start juggling! Remember to keep your eyes on the ball — up and down, up and down.

- Toss the ball up into the air — your hand goes flat.
- Catch the ball in your other hand — your hand curves down as you catch it.
- Toss it up again.
- Now try this with two or three balls! Oh, no! You dropped one!

Wall Games

Mimes are masters at making walls appear out of thin air — and finding a surprise on the other side!

Push Over!

Imagine there's a wall — right there in front of you.

- Touch the wall — your hands snap flat against it.
- Slide both hands along the wall.

- Why not try to push your wall over? Use your shoulders and hips.

Knock, Knock! Who's There?

Find a good mime partner! You and your partner stand on the opposite sides of an imaginary wall. Don't look at each other!

- Both of you explore the wall — from top to bottom.
- Listen! Someone is knocking on the other side of the wall.
- Better explore that wall again!
- It's time to look over the top — snap your hands over the top of the wall.
- Up on your toes — both of you! Look over the top. Surprise! Are you both scared? Is one of you disappointed? Is the other one in love?

Moving Day!

Get ready for moving day. There are oodles of boxes to lift and move. Some are fat, some are tall and some are really heavy.

Make a Box

- Imagine there's a box — hanging right there in front of you.
- Reach out — keep your hand relaxed.
- Feel one side of the box — snap your hand flat. Feel the other side.
- Pick the box up. It's very wide!

How high is this box?

Stretch and Squeeze

You'll have to move all sorts of boxes. Beware! They can change shape right before your eyes.

- Pick up a medium-sized box.
- Squeeze the sides together. Presto! Now it's a very thin box.

How wide?

- Stretch the top and bottom. Presto chango! Now it's a very, very tall box.
- How tiny can you make it?

Muscle Power

Are you ready to lift the heaviest box? What's in it? Dishes? The TV? Imagine the box is right there — on the floor in front of you. Really see it.

- Explore the box — feel the top and the sides with both hands.
- Stand back. This is going to be a big job!
- Better get started — slip your fingers under the box.
- You need more muscle! Get down on one knee, bend your back, and put your whole body into one mighty heft.

Box Relay

Attention! All mime movers form a line.

Here comes the first box.   Watch out! It's tipping.   This box is really heavy.

25

Rope Tricks

Reach! Pull! Tug! What's at the end of your rope?

Up, Up and Away

There's a rope dangling up there — right over your head.

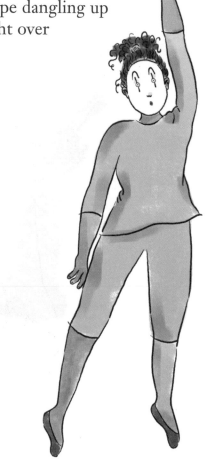

- Reach up, way up — curl your fingers around the rope.
- There's a balloon on the other end. It's pulling your arm up — and now your toes. Happy landing!

Walking the Dog

You have a new puppy, and Rover has never been on a leash before.

- Suddenly, Rover is taking you for a walk — first in one direction, then in the other.
- You're zigzagging around the room — running and walking, starting and stopping.
- Finally, Rover wraps his leash around your legs. Oh! Oh!

Puppet on a String

You are a mime marionette. There are strings attached to your back, head, arms and legs. Is someone — or something — pulling your strings?

- The string attached to your elbow lifts your arm up. It suddenly lets you go.
- Your arm flops down. Your body wobbles.
- Another string pulls your right knee up — and then lets it float slowly back down. Your whole body wobbles.

Calling All Robots!

You are a mechanical being. All your joints are hinged. Stand tall in a rigid robot pose with your arms bent at the elbows. Activate!

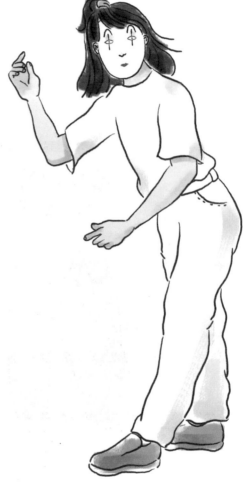

- Your head snaps up — three little jerks to the left, now to the right.
- Your right shoulder snaps up — then your left.
- Your right arm snaps up — your left arm snaps down.
- Check out your hips and legs. Go for a robot walk.

Mime Stories

Are you ready to act out a mime story? Here are a few ideas. Remember: Always start and end in a frozen pose.

Rise and Shine

Good morning!

Stretch. Yawn. Scratch.

Get dressed. Pants, shirt, socks, shoes, hat.

Time to brush those teeth! What a smile!

What time is it? It's late! Gotta go!

Trapped!

You're a mime crouched inside a box. You press against one side. Then another side. Then another. Finally, the last side. You are trapped!

1   Is anyone out there?

2   There must be a way out!

3   What's this? It's a zipper.

4   Free at last!

Investibots of the Cosmos

You are a supersonic Investibot of the Cosmos — in other words, a robot programmed to travel in outer space. Your mission? Explore a distant planet and find the next intergalactic garbage site. Put on your space gear. Check all of your mechanical body parts. Everything is functioning — so far!

- It's all systems go! Blast off! (*Check your instrument panel. Lean way back for blast off.*)

- Hey, this is just like slo mo! (*Move in slow motion.*)
- What's that red light flashing? And that blue one? And the green one? Now everything is flashing! (*Look around your rocket nervously.*)
- Uh-oh! Crash landing ahead! (*Fall down in slow motion and then slowly pick yourself up.*)

- Where am I? (*Look around. Sniff the air. Take a few steps.*)
- There's no gravity here! Whoopee! (*Jump up and down — very slowly.*)
- What's that? Looks like a rope. (*Pick up the end of the rope and give it a yank.*)
- Zowee! There's a box at the end of the rope! Wonder what's in it? (*Carefully open the box and peek inside.*)
- Yuck! There's something really smelly in here! (*Pull something out and quickly toss it away.*)

- Hey! There's something else in here. (*Look in the box again, sniff inside and slowly reach in.*)
- Wow! It's a great big goofy ball! (*Pull out the huge ball and start bouncing it — don't forget there's no gravity!*)

- Ho-hum! All this bouncing makes me sleepy. (*Big yawn.*)
- Think I need a nap! (*Climb inside the box. Curl up. Don't forget to take your great big goofy ball.*)

MASKED PLAY

Fly like a raven. Jitter like a bug. Put on a mask and discover the mysterious character behind each mask you make and wear.

- Make a domino mask.
- Act out an Inuit story.
- Perform a courtly masquerade with your friends.

The World of Mask

What happens when you put on a mask? Does a Frankenstein mask suddenly change you from an everyday kid into a lurching monster?

People have been making and wearing masks since the earliest times. Masked drama has been performed by cultures all over the world, for special ceremonies and rituals and sometimes just for fun.

African Masks

In the Democratic Republic of the Congo, the Quba people wear a ceremonial helmet mask that fits over the head. The mask is made of leather, feathers, shells or even a bell. It is worn for special ceremonies when boys come of age.

North American Masks

The Gitksan of northern British Columbia use masks to help bridge the worlds of humans, animals and spirits. Dancers wearing this raven transformation mask pull strings to reveal a hidden human face mask.

African Masks

North American Mask

34

Japanese Noh Masks

The Noh dance dramas of Japan were first performed by Buddhist monks and entertainers in the seventh century. Even today, Noh actors wear masks made of painted wood. The five basic types of Noh masks are old people, men, women, gods and monsters.

Japanese Noh Masks

Commedia dell'Arte Masks

In sixteenth-century Italy, the half-masks of the commedia dell'arte actors were made out of leather. They had exaggerated features, like the long nose on greedy Pantalone.

Commedia dell'Arte Masks

Behind the Mask

What's behind the mask? You are — with a whole new identity. When your face is hidden behind a mask, nobody knows how old you are, whether you're a girl or a boy, whether you're shy or bold. It's the way you stand, walk and move your head, arms and body that tells the audience who you are and how you feel.

Neutral Mask

A good way to get used to working with a mask is to start with a neutral mask. You can buy these inexpensive plastic masks at most craft stores.

    The neutral mask has no expression. You'll have to use body language to create a character and communicate emotions.

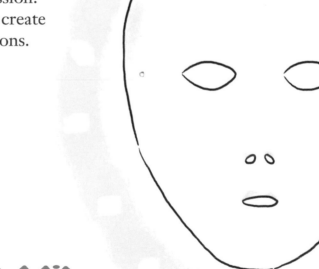

MASK WARNING!

Never touch your mask after you put it on. If you do, you will destroy the illusion.

Putting on Your Mask

- Turn your back to the audience.
- Place the mask on your face.
- Stand neutral.

Working with Your Mask

- Decide on an emotion. Let it show in your shoulders, arms, hands, back, hips and legs.
- When you're ready to act out your character, turn to the audience.
- When you're finished performing, turn your back to the audience, stand neutral and remove your mask.

More Mask Work

With a neutral mask, a bit of imagination and careful body language, you can transform yourself into anyone or anything! Try some character work in your mask.

Mr. Google Takes a Walk

Put your neutral mask on the back of your head and wait for the belly laughs!

- Turn your back to your audience. Bend over so no one sees your head.
- Slip the mask on the back of your head. Stand tall. Do not turn or show your face.
- Walk backward toward the audience — higglety, jigglety style. Step side to side.
- Clasp your hands behind your back.
- Bob up and down.

Get Buggy!

Join the insect world by putting the neutral mask on top of your head.

- Turn your back to your audience. Bend over so no one sees your head.
- Slip the mask on the top of your head.
- Now move like an ancient ant, a spooky spider or a very busy beetle. Don't look up! You don't want the audience to see your face.

Bus Stop

Invite your friends to do this mask scene. Each actor chooses how to wear the mask — on the face, on top of the head or on the back of the head.

Characters

- Nervous Businessman
- Sad Old Lady
- Sneaky Pickpocket
- Pushy Person
- Cool Teenager
- Friendly Dog

Action

A group of people are waiting in line for the bus. They wait and wait. Everybody waits patiently — at first. Then, everyone starts to fidget.

Making Masks

Mask making is a special art. Mask artists use lots of inspiration and imagination to create their magical masks. Here are two kinds of masks you can make to transform yourself.

Domino Mask

A domino mask is a half mask. It only covers your eyes. Try these expressions.

sad

angry

spooky

Raven Mask

You can use this idea to make any kind of bird mask.

What You Need

- file folder or lightweight cardboard
- pencil, ruler and scissors
- string or thin elastic
- color markers or tempera paint and brushes
- feathers, sparkles, stickers, beads, fake fur, etc.

How You Make It

1 Cut out a strip from the file folder, about 40 cm (15 in.) long and 25 cm (10 in.) wide.

2 To add a nose, a snout or a beak, follow this pattern.

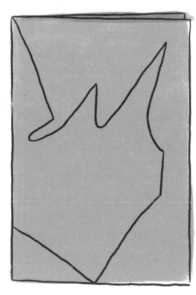

3 Open the mask and bend the nose over. You need to reverse the fold.

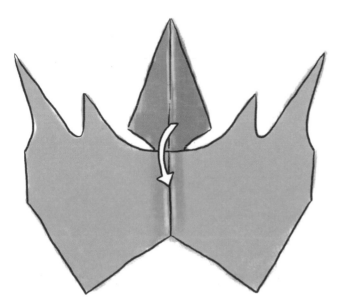

4 To make eyeholes, fold the mask in half and mark the center point. Measure 3 cm ($1\frac{1}{4}$ in.) in both directions from the center mark. Cut out circles about 1.5 cm ($\frac{1}{2}$ in.) in diameter. You may need to make the holes longer or larger.

5 Poke holes in each side of the mask and thread the string or elastic through.

6 Add color and decorations (beads or feathers) to create your own magical raven character.

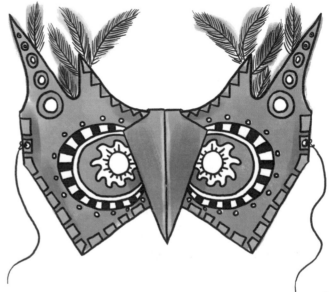

Stick Mask

Some Native North Americans made totem poles with carvings of animal spirits, but the Inuit made totem stick masks. Totem masks have a carved central face of the totem surrounded by smaller totem carvings. The Inuit believed that their masks brought good luck to the wearers.

Owl Stick Mask

Here's a totem mask full of wisdom.

What You Need

- large dinner plate and pencil
- sheet of bristol board
- scissors, masking tape, glue
- small tree branch or stick
- color markers or tempera paint and brushes
- feathers, sparkles, stickers, beads, fake fur, etc.

How You Make It

1 Use the dinner plate to trace two circles on the bristol board. Cut them out.

2 Draw your owl totem on one circle. Tape the stick to the back for a handle.

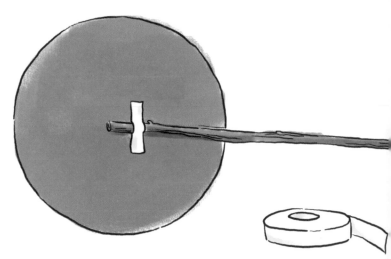

3 Cut five strips of bristol board, 30 cm (12 in.) long and 4 cm (1 $\frac{1}{2}$ in.) wide.

4 Choose an image for your owl. It could be a star to represent the night or a feather. Make a pattern of the image. Trace the pattern five times onto the bristol board and cut each one out. Color and decorate them. Tape each one to a strip of bristol board.

Endangered Species Mask

5 Tape the strips around your totem circle. Glue the other circle on the back of your mask to hold everything in place.

STICK MASK TIPS!

Hold the mask up to your face with one hand. There are no eye holes, so you'll have to look at your feet and to the sides to see where you are going. Use your body to walk, fly, skip or swim like your totem spirit.

The Lost Ring

Here's a short play for lots of different masked characters. Imagine you have been invited to a masquerade ball. Will you be a clown, a young girl or something ghostly and strange? Add a scarf, shawl or hat to give more depth to your character. This play needs a king, queen, clown, bird, miser, young lady, knight and guests.

The characters enter the ballroom one at a time and bow before the king and queen.

- The guests greet each other by bowing, waving or shaking hands.
- Suddenly the clown spots a ring lying on the ground.
- The clown does a merry dance around the ring, then picks it up when no one is looking.

- Before the clown can run away, a mean old miser makes the clown hand the ring over.

- By now everyone sees what is going on. A young lady comes up to the miser and gently holds out her hand.
- The miser tries to walk away in one direction, but the guests stop him. He tries the other direction and again is stopped.
- At last, the miser gives the ring to the girl who puts the ring on her finger.
- A knight enters, bows before the young girl and kisses the hand with the ring.
- Everyone celebrates with great joy.
- Freeze. Hold for five seconds. Stand neutral. Exit.

Owl and Raven

This Inuit story tells us how Raven became black. One person is the narrator and reads the story. The other two players don masks and silently perform the story.

You need one mask for Owl and two masks for Raven, one white mask and onc black mask. The players should be dressed in white. At the end of the story, Raven wears a long black cloak or coat.

NARRATOR: Long ago in the land of endless snow, Owl and Raven were the best of friends.

(Owl and Raven fly in together, jumping and playing. Raven wears a white mask.)

NARRATOR: Raven had a gift for Owl. He had made her a beautiful white and black cloak to wear.

(Raven and Owl mime putting the cloak on Owl.)

NARRATOR: Owl was so delighted that she gave Raven a pair of boots made out of whale bone.

(Raven and Owl mime putting boots on Raven.)

NARRATOR: Owl also had a white cloak for Raven to wear. But every time she tried to give it to him, he would hop about, first on one foot, then on the other.

(Raven mimes hopping about. Owl acts frustrated and upset.)

NARRATOR: Raven would not sit still. Owl was very upset, "Sit still," she hooted, "or I will pour this black lamp oil all over you."

(*Raven keeps hopping about.*)

NARRATOR: Owl could not stand it one moment longer. She took the lamp and poured the oil all over Raven.

(*Owl mimes pouring oil over Raven. Raven puts on the black mask and a black cloak.*)

NARRATOR: "Qaq! Quq!" cried Raven. Since that day, Raven has been black all over.

(*Raven and Owl fly off in different directions.*)

CLOWNING AROUND

Everybody loves a clown. Get in touch with your funny bone and invent your own "funtastical" clown. Take a walk in a pair of flippity-floppity shoes. Sneeze confetti. Ha-Ha-Chooo! Now mop up the mess with a never-ending hankie. Let the clowning begin!

- Discover your clown hat.
- Fall on your face.
- Make a flower squirt.

Send in the Clowns

Clowns have kept the world in stitches for thousands of years. Court jesters clowned for the pharaohs of ancient Egypt and the emperors of ancient China. Clowning fools appeared in Shakespeare's plays in the sixteenth century. In the American Southwest, Hopi clowns still carry on the old tradition of providing comic relief during important rituals and ceremonies.

The first step in turning yourself into a clown is deciding what kind of clown you want to be. Here are three main kinds of clowns to choose from. They have different styles of makeup and costumes, different personalities and different ways of making people laugh.

White-Face Pierrot

Pierrot is a classic white-face clown. Wide eyes and a slap-happy grin stand out on his completely white face. Pierrot dresses splendidly in bright colors and a cone hat. At first glance, he appears gentle and charming. Don't be taken in by his grand manners, though — this bossy, mischievous clown is always getting in and out of trouble.

Zany Auguste

Everything about Auguste is exaggerated — bright red nose, huge grin, fuzzy hair, baggy pants, enormous shoes, squirting flowers. Nothing seems to go right for this simple, clumsy clown who is everyone's best friend and worst enemy at the same time. Even a squirting flower backfires and hits poor Auguste in the eye.

Lonely Tramp

There is no mistaking the sad-looking Lonely Tramp. He wears simple makeup, his clothes are patched and tattered, and his luck goes from bad to worse.

Charlie Chaplin based his Little Tramp clown on the poor people he had seen living in the slums of London, England. Later, Little Tramp became one of the most lovable characters of the silent movies.

Hattitude

Discover your clown by finding your hat first! A hat gives you personality and attitude. It tells you who you are and how you feel. First, you'll need to gather a collection of all sorts of different hats.

Mirror Mugging

Sit in front of a mirror and put a hat on your head. Settle into your hat and let it help you explore your clown character.

Hat Tricks

Your hat can become almost anything! Hold it in your hands and watch it transform itself — and you!

- Steer it.
- Baby it.

Smile!

Frown!

Walking the Walk

Every clown walks a special walk. Some shuffle, some slip-slide and some bob up and down. Here are some ways to help you find your clown walk.

Hat Walk

Plop a hat on your head and let it take you for a walk. Exaggerate all your movements.

- Does a top hat make you strut?
- Does a teeny-tiny hat make you tiptoe?

Animal Walk

Think of an animal and how it moves. Try these walks on for size:

- a chicken darting around
- a duck waddling
- an ape taking big steps and swinging its arms

Add Attitude!

How does your animal move if it's feeling on top of the world? How about down in the dumps?

Get Dressed

Make amazing clown costumes out of old clothes lying around the house or things you pick up at a second-hand store. Look for bright colors and bold patterns. Nothing has to fit!

Baggy Pants

Find some old trousers that are miles too big and make some baggy pants!

What You Need

- old trousers
- scissors
- wire or opened coat hanger
- strong tape
- thread and needle
- suspenders

How You Make Them

1 Undo a few stitches in the hem of the waistband. Thread stiff wire or opened coat hanger through the hem.

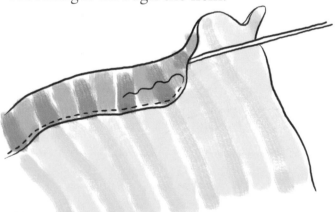

2 Tape the two ends of the wire together. Stitch the hem closed.

3 Jump into your baggy pants and attach suspenders to hold them up.

Floppy Shoes

Some clowns wear shoes the size of shovels. Can't find any big enough? Here's how to make your own.

What You Need

- large piece of cardboard
- pencil
- scissors
- colored markers
- tape

How You Make Them

1 Place your shoes on the cardboard, and draw a much larger foot shape around each shoe. Cut out your shoes.

2 At each ankle, cut out a U-shape to make tabs.

3 Color your shoes. Are they dressy, worn, fancy or plain? Maybe your toes stick out — better draw toenails.

4 Put the cardboard shoes on top of your own shoes and wrap the tabs around your ankles. Tape the tabs together. Now go for a goofy walk!

Find Your Face

It's time to try on a clown face. Before you start experimenting with makeup, you might want to sketch some ideas. Do you want eyebrows that go up and a mouth that turns down? How about a star on your cheek? Freckles across your nose?

Clown Makeup

Clown makeup is best when it is kept simple. If you have an allergy to face paint, just dust your face with baby powder or white flour.

What You Need

- mirror
- shower cap or baseball cap
- white or flesh-colored face paint for base
- cotton balls
- baby powder or face powder
- black eyebrow pencil
- red lipstick or red face paint

Making Up

1 Cover your hair with a shower cap or an old baseball cap.

2 Use your fingertips to spread the base makeup all over your face.

3 Using cotton balls or tissues, wipe the makeup off any areas that you want to paint over, such as your nose or mouth.

4 Lightly powder your face (this helps the makeup stay put).

5 Use the eyebrow pencil to draw in eyebrows, add freckles or outline your mouth.

7 Add special features to make your clown unique. (You can buy a big red nose or make one using an egg carton.)

6 Use the lipstick to make a red nose, fill in your smile or make your cheeks rosy.

8 When you're finished, powder your face again.

Gimmicks and Gags

All clowns need goofy gimmicks. Here are two classic clown gimmicks you can make yourself.

Never-Ending Hankie

Tie five or six — or ten or twelve — hankies or scarves together at the corners. Add a surprise on the end. Then stuff them into a deep pocket or up a big sleeve.

You're suddenly feeling very, very sad. Tears start to fall. Your nose starts to run. Sniff! Snivel!

You need a hankie! Slowly start pulling out your hankie — sniveling, sniffing and honking all the while.

The Big Sneeze

Stuff confetti in a hankie and tuck it into your pocket. Oh, dear! You have to sneeze. Reach into your pocket and pull out a hankie. Ha-ha-ha-CHOO!

Squirting Flower

Be sure to use this gimmick when your audience least expects it.

What You Need

- large nail
- empty plastic lemon
- plastic straw
- crepe paper
- scissors
- glue

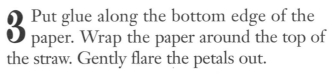

How You Make It

1 Use the nail to make a hole beside the screw top of the plastic lemon. Put the plastic straw in the hole.

2 Cut a strip of crepe paper 32 cm (about 12 $\frac{1}{2}$ in.) long. Fold the crepe paper like an accordion. Cut out a petal shape and unfold the paper.

3 Put glue along the bottom edge of the paper. Wrap the paper around the top of the straw. Gently flare the petals out.

4 Fill the lemon with water and place it in your breast pocket. Invite another clown to smell your beautiful flower!

Clown Foolery

Think of some silly actions to make your clown come alive. Dance with a broom. Wear your shoe as a hat. Hug a chair.

Goofing Around

Put yourself in the shoes of a rock star or an athlete. Settle in. Add lots of attitude and personality. Don't forget to exaggerate your actions.

Just imagine …

… lifting weights when you are out of shape.

… dancing with a friendly broom.

Clown Falls

There is a real art to falling and not hurting yourself. The trick is to be completely in control while looking as if you are completely out of control. Try falling on a mat or rug first, and then take it step by step.

Face First

Bottom First

- Bend your knees and lean way back.
- Land on your bottom — not your back — and roll gently backward.
- Put your hands on the floor behind you to stop yourself. Grin.

- Start off walking your silly clown walk. Catch the toe of your right foot behind the heel of your left foot.
- Make it look as if you are about to fall forward. Put your hands on the floor and a foot in the air.
- Lower yourself down with your arms and lie with your face flat on the floor. Look up and giggle.

Clown Scenes: Solo

Ready to get your clown act together? Try these scenes, and then make up some of your own. Practice your scenes first, and then find an audience. It's show time under the Big Tent!

Squeaky Toy

Pretend you've got a toy at the end of a string. Off you go.

- What's that squeaky noise? Stop. Turn and look around. Gesture for your toy to be quiet.
- Pull again. Stop again. Pull again. Stop again. Pull again. Stop again.
- What do you do? Pick it up? Plug your ears? Keep walking?

What a Mess!

There's a big mess of paper all over the floor. Oh, my! Better pick it all up.

- Tuck a wastebasket under your arm. Stoop down and pick up a paper. P-U-L-L!
- Oh, no! All the pieces are stuck! You P-U-L-L them up, one at a time.
- When you bend over to pick up the last piece, the whole kit and kaboodle falls on the floor.
- You pick the mess up again. It spills again.
- Oh, well! That's a clown's life.

Get That Ball!

The ball game is over and your team has won.

- Give your teammates high fives. Wave good-bye.
- Suddenly, you see the ball on the ground.
- As you lean over to pick it up, your foot kicks it away.

- That's weird. Try again. The ball scoots in another direction.
- Quick. Grab it. No luck!
- Sneak attack. It gets away again.
- What do you do? Tackle it? Sit on it? Give up?

Clown Scenes: **Partners**

There's only one thing better than a clown — and that's two clowns.

Bossy and Zip have a simple job to do — mopping the floor. Unfortunately, nothing is simple and easy with Zip around!

For props, you need a bucket filled with confetti and a mop. When playing this scene, remember your clown falls, use your mime skills and speak only gibberish — no real words allowed! Read through the scene first, then start clowning.

Bossy and Zip

BOSSY *enters carrying the bucket.*

ZIP *follows behind carrying a mop over his shoulder.*

BOSSY *tells* ZIP *to mop the floor.*

ZIP *turns to mop the floor and hits* BOSSY *on the back of the head.*

BOSSY *gets angry and orders* ZIP *to mop again.*

ZIP *hits* BOSSY *on the back of the head again. Oops!*

ZIP *freezes with fear.*

BOSSY *shows* ZIP *how to use the mop.*

ZIP *starts to copy* BOSSY. *Then — whammo! —* ZIP *plops the mop in* BOSSY'S *face and knocks her down.*

ZIP *tries to help* BOSSY *get up.*

BOSSY *pushes* ZIP *away and picks up the bucket.*

BOSSY *chases* ZIP *around.*

BOSSY *gets ready to toss a bucket of water on* ZIP.

ZIP *ducks — and the confetti hits the audience.*

BOSSY *and* ZIP *laugh and hug each other, and then exit.*

DANCE DRAMA

**Stretch! Swing! Bounce! Leap! Go fast. Go slow.
Up high. Down low. You can tell amazing stories by how
you shape and move your body. Get ready to dance up a storm!**

- Write your name in the sky.
- Freeze into an ice sculpture.
- Step inside a dance sack.

Jump for Joy!

We dance to tell stories, celebrate occasions and express ideas and beliefs. Mostly we dance just because it feels so good!

"Dance is your body singing," someone once said. That's a good description of what people have been doing all over the world and all through the ages.

Isadora Duncan

Born in San Francisco in 1877, Isadora Duncan studied ballet as a child. She wore a tight-fitting tutu and toe-pinching slippers and practiced the precise steps of classical ballet. Later, Isadora was inspired by the natural and free-flowing dance of the ancient Greeks. She donned a loose, flowing tunic, bared her feet and created a style of dance based on everyday movements — running, jumping, leaping, twirling. This was the beginning of modern dance.

Classical Indian Dance

In Hindu temples, dancing girls make picture gestures with their hands. They are called mudras. The dancer uses her hands to make a fish swim, a bird fly and a flower bloom. What a wonderful way to tell a story without words.

Ballet

Ballet is just over 400 years old. King Louis XIV of France loved to invite people to dance at his palace in Versailles. In 1653, he performed as the rising sun in Le ballet de la nuit.

Music Maestro!

Dancers usually move to music. Whether it is the sound of a drum or a symphony orchestra, music provides a beat or rhythm to move to.

Some dancers have danced to the sounds of the world around us — the humming of insects or the whooshes of traffic. Some dancers have used poetry as a background for dance. Others have used silence.

Your Music

The dance floor is yours! Why not experiment with different kinds of music — classical, jazz, rock and roll, folk, country and western? Explore how each style of music makes you move differently.

Musical Movement

Here's a series of movements you can try with different styles of music. Relax and feel the music with your body.

Rag Doll

Hang over at the waist. Plant your feet apart. Bend your knees. Hang your head. Let your arms flop forward.

- Slowly start to curl up from the base of the spine, one vertebra at a time.
- Slowly move your shoulders and then your head up.

Dance Sack

Find or make a stretchy sack, big enough to crawl inside. Put on some music and explore your sack.

- Lie on your back and reach out as far as you can.
- Scrunch up in a little ball.
- Discover your own way of moving about the room. Is it in tall, tiny steps or low, slow slithers?

Find Your Space

Look up. Look down. Look at the space around you.

Exploring Directions

Here are some games that will help you explore the space above you, around you and below you.

Goofy Ball

Imagine you are tossing an invisible ball. Follow it with your head.

- It hits the wall on your right. Then your left.
- It bounces on the floor under your feet. On the ceiling over your head.
- Boing! It zigzags from one corner to another.

The Passing Parade

The parade is coming! You can hear it, but you can't see it.

- Look way up, over the heads of the crowd. You still can't see!
- Crouch down and peer between everyone's elbows. Still no luck!
- Get down on your belly and slither your way to the front of the crowd. You make it just in time to see everything!

Find Your Pace

Speed up. Slow down. How quickly or slowly you move creates the pace of your dance.

Exploring Pace

When you change the pace of your dance, you change how you communicate your ideas.

Led by a String

Pretend you're a puppet with invisible strings. Somebody starts pulling your strings, one by one.

- The string attached to your nose is pulling you. You zigzag across the room, first at a walk, then at a run!
- The string attached to your elbow is pulling you. Away you go — fast then slow, spinning and twirling around.

Exploring Energy

When you change the kind of energy you use, you change the meaning of your dance.

Wet Noodle Walk

Start relaxed and still, like a wet noodle. Now off you go!

- Imagine you are as tall as a giraffe. Whip about the room.
- You are as heavy as an elephant and really short. Go for a lumpy, slow walk.
- You are as square as a box and as rigid as a rock. Cross the room.

Moving On!

Dance your way through these games. Use your whole body, and feel each shape and motion you're creating.

The World's Greatest!

"Ladies and gentlemen, your attention, please!" Presenting ...

- The world's greatest boxer!

- The world's greatest pizza maker!
- The world's greatest sword fighter!

Slo-Mo Tumble

You are a sculpture made of ice. The sun is shining, and you are slowly starting to melt.

- Start bending your knees and shrinking.

- Plop onto your bottom. (It is the best padding you have for a safe landing.)
- Place your hands on the floor, and spread out in one huge puddle.

Jungle Journey

There's a dense and scary jungle standing between you and home. Watch for kid-eating creatures as you make your way through the twisted vines.

- Push the branches out of the way.

- Crawl under hanging branches.

- You reach the clearing. It is a swamp filled with alligators. You'll have to get across!
- It'll take two huge leaps. Don't fall in!

- Step over fallen trees.

Shapes and Patterns

Dance is all about physical shapes and movement patterns. A choreographer creates a dance by using a combination of shapes and patterns to express something or to tell a story. Here are some games to get you into shape! Choose some favorite shapes and put them together into a simple pattern.

Sky Writing

Imagine you're flying. Write your name in the bright blue sky using your arms to make big, swinging motions.

Sand Writing

Imagine you're at the beach. Use your feet to write your name in the sand in huge, flowing letters.

Cat Writing

Pretend you're a cat. Stretch out into a cat pose, and shape the letters of your name using your whole body.

Gadget Kid

Turn yourself into a noisy gadget. Create a movement that you can repeat over and over. Add a sound that matches your move, like blip, sproing or whee.

Group Gears

Find some other gadget kids and move together! The first player chooses a level — high, medium or low — and keeps repeating a movement, including sound effects. The second player joins in, moving at a different level and adding a different sound effect. Then the third player joins in, and so on.

When all the gadgets are moving together, the leader picks up the pace and the others follow. Then it's time to gear down. Everyone moves slower and slower until all the gears have stopped.

Outer Space

What if you and a friend land in outer space where there isn't enough gravity to hold you down? All of your moves are in slow motion. You and your partner move in and around each other without telling each other what to do and without touching.

FIRST DANCER: Choose a shape and freeze.
SECOND DANCER: Fill in the space. Freeze.

FIRST DANCER: Slowly move out of your shape. Make a different shape. Freeze.
SECOND DANCER: Fill in the space. Freeze.

Maypole

Get a dozen friends together and celebrate spring with a maypole dance. In this circular folk dance, the dancers move together and weave patterns with the ribbons.

Making the Maypole

Ask an adult to help erect your maypole.

What You Need

- a cardboard carpet tube, 2.5 m (8 ft.) high
- 12 ribbons at least 4.5 m (15 ft.) long in three different colors
- folk music

Alternating the three colors, attach the ribbons to the pole near the top. Erect the pole.

Let's Dance!

Turn on the music and dance.

- Each dancer holds out the end of a ribbon at shoulder height and faces the pole.
- The first dancer turns to face left, the second dancer turns to face right, the third dancer turns to the left, the fourth dancer turns to the right, and so on.
- Each group starts moving slowly, in opposite directions around the pole.
  - When half of the pole is wrapped with ribbon, the two groups reverse and unwind.

Metamorphosis

Butterflies go through metamorphosis, changing from an egg into a caterpillar into a cocoon and, finally, transforming into a butterfly. In this dance drama, you tell the story of metamorphosis with your creative movements. Choose music that is gentle and joyful, and tuck colorful scarves into the arms of your shirt so you can use them for the flight of the butterfly.

- Curl up, as small as possible.
- Slowly reach out with one arm, and feel around. Suddenly pull it in.
- Reach out with the other arm in a different direction. Pull it in.
- Gently move your shoulders and your back.
- Stretch one leg out and then one arm.

- Look up and all around. The world looks amazing! Are you afraid or very curious?
- Crawl slowly along the floor. Reach up. Crawl. Reach up and crawl.

- Move slowly to a rag doll position, knees bent slightly and head hanging toward the floor.
- Move slowly to a standing position. Begin spinning a magical web all around yourself.
- Hold this position for a few seconds, then burst free. Pull the scarves out.
- Suddenly you are swooping and flitting about the room. Reach high and low. Spin and swirl.
- Leap and bounce. Enjoy all the wonders of flight.
- Now the butterfly is tired. Move back into a rag doll, then curl up on the floor with your beautiful scarves lying on the floor around you.

ACT II: SOUND ADVICE

In this act, you get to be an invisible actor. You'll be telling stories and creating scenes using just your voice, sound effects and some wonderful puppets. Get ready to exercise your vocal cords as you explore ...

- Puppets and Puppetry
- Readers' Theater
- Radio Plays

PUPPETS AND PUPPETRY

Make a glove dance and a sock talk. Teach an accordion puppet to swim. Challenge a fellow puppeteer to a tongue-twisting duel. All this is possible in the wonderful world of puppets.

- Learn how to be a puppeteer.
- Create your own puppet theater.
- Put on a real puppet play.

World of Puppetry

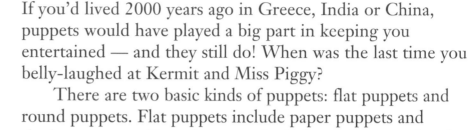

If you'd lived 2000 years ago in Greece, India or China, puppets would have played a big part in keeping you entertained — and they still do! When was the last time you belly-laughed at Kermit and Miss Piggy?

There are two basic kinds of puppets: flat puppets and round puppets. Flat puppets include paper puppets and shadow puppets. Round puppets include marionettes, hand puppets and rod puppets. Both kinds of puppets have been around for thousands of years.

One-Person Puppet Show

In China, there is a popular street puppet theater operated by one person. The Ku Li Tzu puppeteer carries the puppet stage on a pole. A long robe hides the puppeteer's body from the audience. At show time, the pole is placed on the ground, and the back of the stage leans against a wall. Both round and flat puppets appear on this stage.

Mr. Punch

This humpbacked hand puppet with the hooked nose is both a coward and a terrible bully. He arrived in England in the seventeenth century from Italy, where he was called Pulcinella. When he arrived in Germany, he acquired the name Hans Wurst (Jack Sausage). In Holland, he was called Hans Pickle Herring.

Bunraku

The stars of a Bunraku performance — a Japanese puppetry tradition that dates back to the seventeenth century — are puppets half the size of an adult. It takes three puppeteers to operate one puppet. The chief puppeteer, dressed in a colorful costume, holds the puppet in front and controls the puppet's head with the left hand and its right arm with the right hand. The other two puppeteers dress completely in black and wear gauze face masks. One moves a hand and the other moves the feet.

Stick Puppets

Here are some quick and easy ways you and your friends can make a whole cast of puppets for your own stick puppet play.

Draw a character (human, animal or mechanical) on a piece of bristol board. Paint or color it. Or dress it up by gluing on fabric or felt clothes and yarn for hair or fur. Tape a popsicle stick, bamboo stick or chopstick to the back of the puppet.

Cut out magazine pictures and turn them into a puppet. Try a different head and body, like a baby's head on an elephant's body!

To make the puppet stiff, glue the pictures to a piece of bristol board. Cut out the puppet and tape a popsicle stick, bamboo stick or chopstick to the back.

Cut out one of your school pictures. Draw your body on a piece of bristol board. How about your head on the body of a weight lifter? Glue the head and body to a piece of bristol board. Cut out the puppet and tape a stick to the back.

Dueling Stick Puppets

Here's a good way to find your puppet's distinctive voice. Challenge a fellow puppeteer to a duel of tongue twisters. Start off slowly and then get faster and faster. For more fun, act out your favorite tongue twister — at normal speed!

A Skunk Stunk

A skunk sat on a stump.
The skunk thunk the stump stunk,
But the stump thunk the skunk stunk.

I Thought

I thought a thought,
But the thought I thought
Was not the thought
I thought I thought.

Slippery One-Liner

Six slippery snails slid slowly seaward.

Stick Puppeteering

Get your friends together and choose a folktale to perform. Make puppets for all the characters, and don't forget to make the props. Construct a puppet theater (see pages 96–97). Choose a simple story, such as "The Three Billy Goats Gruff." Make a script for the characters and practice first in front of a mirror.

89

Hand Puppets

Almost anything that you can slip on your hand can become a hand puppet. Use whatever you can find — gloves, mittens, socks, even paper bags.

Glove Puppet

Here's a hands-on puppet that's easy to make.

What You Need

- craft knife
- tennis ball
- googley eyes, bead, piece of felt
- markers, glue
- glove

How You Make It

1 Ask an adult to cut an X into the bottom of the tennis ball.

2 Glue on the eyes and the bead for a nose. Add a felt mouth and maybe a mustache and fuzzy hair.

3 Put the glove on and then place the tennis ball head on your pointer finger.

Puppeteering

Here are some ways that you can hold your hand puppet.

Oh, I love ice cream.

I didn't do it.

Look out!

Onward and upward.

Tall Tales for Two to Tell

Find a puppeteering friend and try these tall tales together. Each puppet takes turns making up a one-liner tall tale, then another, and another … Practice a bit, and then try it on the stage of the puppet theater (see pages 96–97).

Down on the Farm

PUPPET 1: On my farm, the corn grows so tall that at night I can climb all the way up to the moon.

PUPPET 2: On my farm, the chickens are so smart that they lay eggs and then scramble them for my breakfast.

Fortunately/Unfortunately

PUPPET 1: Just this week, my family won a trip to a tropical island.

PUPPET 2: Unfortunately, I got the measles.

PUPPET 1: Fortunately, the trip was postponed for a month.

PUPPET 2: Unfortunately, there was a hurricane.

PUPPET 1: Fortunately, it missed our island.

Rod Puppets

Rod puppets have moving parts attached to rods or sticks. A puppeteer uses both hands to operate these puppets!

Accordion Fish Puppet

Make this simple rod puppet and take it for a swim.

What You Need

- a strip of corrugated cardboard
- scissors
- tape, glue
- paint, ribbons, glitter
- 2 bamboo sticks

How You Make It

1 On the cardboard, draw the outline of a fish, about 40 cm (16 in.) long. Make sure that the ribs of the cardboard run from the top to the bottom of your fish.

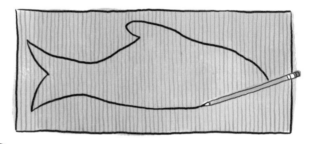

2 Cut out the fish, then paint and decorate it.

3 Attach one stick to the tail and the other to the head of the fish.

Princess Puppet

Here's a rod puppet that has a 3-D head and a real gown.

What You Need

- head-sized Styrofoam ball
- wool yarn, bead, googley eyes, paints, glue
- scissors
- piece of felt, ribbon
- dowel and bamboo stick
- tape or glue

How You Make It

1 Turn the Styrofoam ball into a head by painting it and adding some features — maybe a beady nose, wooly hair, googley eyes and a hat. Stick the head onto the dowel.

2 Cut a circle out of the felt that's big enough to fit the body of your puppet. Cut a small circle out of the center big enough to slip the dowel through. You can add hands and feet made from felt.

3 Slip the felt gown onto the dowel. Wind and tie the ribbon around the neck opening to secure it.

4 Attach the bamboo stick to one hand of the puppet.

Jointed Jester

Your jester can have more than one moving part, maybe an arm and maybe a leg.

What You Need

- cardboard
- pencil, scissors
- round-head fasteners
- 3 thin dowels or bamboo sticks about 40 cm (16 in.) long
- masking tape

How You Make It

1 On the cardboard, draw an outline of the body, neck and head of the jester. It should be about 20 cm (8 in.) tall. Draw the legs with feet (about 20 cm or 8 in.) long. Draw arms with hands (about 14 cm or $5\frac{1}{2}$ in.). If you want joints at the elbows and knees, make each limb in two sections. Cut out the pieces.

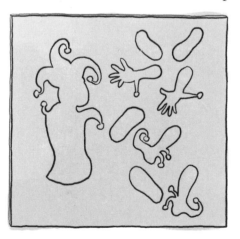

2 Attach the arms to the shoulders and the legs to the hips with round-head fasteners. Attach fasteners to the movable joints.

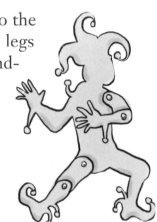

3 Attach one dowel or stick to the back of the neck of your puppet. Attach one rod to a hand and the other to a foot.

Rod Puppet Puppeteering

Jest for fun!

No applause —
just throw coins.

Tiptoe and off I go.

Puppet Theaters

It's time to put on a puppet play! Here are some ideas for easy-to-make puppet theaters.

Theater in a Box

Here's a simple puppet theater that works for all sorts of puppets. You might want to ask an adult to help with the construction.

What You Need

- large cardboard box
- scissors or utility knife
- large nail
- dowel or bamboo stick (a bit longer than the width of the box)
- black piece of fabric

How You Make It

1 Remove the flaps from a large cardboard box.

2 Cut a square hole in the bottom, leaving a border of 8–10 cm (3–4 in.) on all sides.

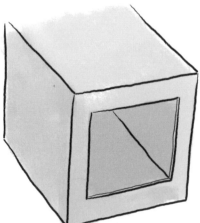

3 Use a large nail to make a hole in each side of the box, 10.5 cm (4 in.) from the back of the box. Insert the dowel.

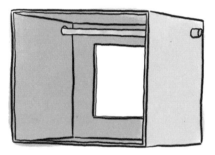

4 To make a stage curtain, drape the piece of fabric over the dowel. Use tape to keep the curtain in place. Instead of a curtain, you can create your own background on a piece of cardboard and tape it to the dowel.

Show time — open the curtain.

A Movable Stage

Here's a stage you can carry around. It works best with hand puppets.

What You Need

- saucer, pencil
- shallow cardboard box
- utility knife
- two lengths of cord, each 90 cm (about 36 in.) long
- paint, decorations

How You Make It

1 Use the saucer to draw two circles on the bottom of the box. Ask an adult to cut out the circles and to make four holes in the sides of the box where the cords go through.

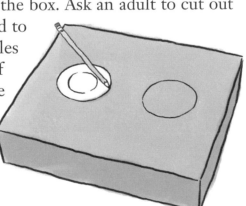

2 Slip the cords through the holes in the sides and knot the end of each one. Make sure the cords are long enough to fit comfortably around your neck.

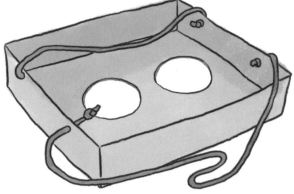

3 Decorate your theater any way that strikes your fancy.

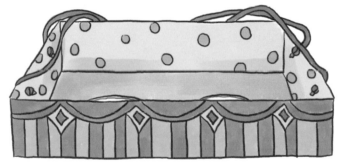

4 Slip the cords over your head and pop your puppets through the holes.

Growing Wings

A Chinese folk tale adapted by Deborah Dunleavy
For this play, you and your friends get to have lots of fun
making rod puppets for all the characters and stick puppets
for all the props. Here's what you need.

The Cast

The Props

- Three narrators (they can be puppets, too)
- Goose girl
- Flock of geese
- Landowner's daughter
- Merchant's daughter
- Magistrate's daughter
- Princess
- Spirit of wings

- pond
- trees
- sun

- mountains
- crescent moon

The Play

FIRST NARRATOR: Over by the duck pond, a peasant's daughter was feeding some geese.

(*Goose Girl appears.*)

SECOND NARRATOR: Her head was bowed down, and she was crying. The geese just honked and honked. They paid no attention to her.

GEESE: Honk! Honk!

THIRD NARRATOR: Just then, the land-owner's daughter came along. She saw Goose Girl sobbing and rubbing her eyes.

(*Enter Landowner's Daughter.*)

LANDOWNER'S DAUGHTER: What is the matter?

GOOSE GIRL: I wish I had wings.

LANDOWNER'S DAUGHTER: That's very strange. Why would you want wings?

GOOSE GIRL: If I had wings, I could fly. I could fly above the trees, over the hills, beyond the mountains and right up to the face of the moon.

LANDOWNER'S DAUGHTER: That is the silliest thing I have ever heard. Everyone knows that girls can't fly. Besides, you are only a goose girl. If anyone should get wings, it's me!

FIRST NARRATOR: Soon the landowner's daughter started to think that growing wings might be fun. She turned her face to the sun, opened her arms wide and waited for wings to grow.

SECOND NARRATOR: The merchant's daughter did the same thing.

(Enter Merchant's Daughter.)

MERCHANT'S DAUGHTER: I want to grow wings, too.

THIRD NARRATOR: And the magistrate's daughter …

(Enter Magistrate's Daughter.)

MAGISTRATE'S DAUGHTER: I wish I had wings so I could fly.

ALL NARRATORS: Even the princess wanted to have wings.

(Enter Princess.)

PRINCESS: I must have wings.

First Narrator: When the spirit of wings saw that all the children were waiting for wings to grow, it flew down to speak to them.

(Spirit of Wings appears from behind the mountain. The children gather together.)

Spirit of Wings: Only one child shall have wings.

All the Children: I want wings! I want wings! Please, let me have wings!

Spirit of Wings: Quiet! Goose Girl shall have wings for she was the first to ask.

(Goose Girl disappears and a bird replaces her. The bird flies up into the air as all the children watch.)

Children: Good-bye, Goose Girl. Good-bye.

Landowner's Daughter: Wow! She really can fly. She is almost as high as the moon.

(A crescent moon appears.)

READERS' THEATER

No costumes. No props. No scenery. No lines to memorize. No kidding! This kind of drama is called Readers' (or Readers or Reader's) Theater — RT, for short. You can perform RT solo or with a cast of friends.

- Build a streetscape with words.
- Read flea-training instructions.
- Perform an African folk tale.

103

Readers' Roots

Readers' Theater got its start with the "beat" (as in "beatnik") generation of the 1950s and 1960s. College students read plays and poetry in coffeehouses — a "cool" thing to do. Today, playwrights sometimes use Readers' Theater to hear how their plays sound before they hit the stage.

Word Power

In Readers' Theater, the words of the script are everything. A poem or story — real or imagined — has the power to cast a spell over an audience. Listeners leave the here and now behind and step inside the world the words create. They can travel through time and to distant shores. They can wrestle with tigers, live the life of an acrobat or flee from a fiery volcano.

Keep It Simple

RT players are actually readers, and their performance focuses on the words of the script. It's important not to upstage the script with fancy sets and costumes or big gestures. Here's how to keep it simple.

- The readers read the script without jumping around or hamming it up.
- The players "dress down" so they won't distract the audience. They wear simple tunics or T-shirts and pants.
- The script is always on the stage, either sitting on a lectern or held in the hands of the players.
- The set needs just a few stools for the players to perch on; a music stand or lectern for the script; a black curtain or screen for a backdrop.

Hear Ye! Hear Ye!

Before you tackle RT head on, give your voice a workout. Pretend your audience is filling a huge auditorium. You'll have to throw your voice to the very back of the hall. That's called projection. Try these workouts.

Selling Newspapers

You are selling newspapers at a newsstand. Shout out these headlines:

Killer tomato takes over Texas!
Giant centipede stampedes picnic!

Advertising Apples

You are selling your goods in an olden-day market. Advertise your wares:

Fresh red apples, shiny and bright —
Buy one! Buy one!
Buy one tonight!
Lettuce and carrots —
For just one nickel.
Buy a cucumber —
A cucumber pickle.

Ladies and Gentlemen!

You are the ringmaster in the circus. It's time to announce the next act:

Ladies and gentlemen —
Look way up!
See the amazing Grizelda
Swing through the air —
On the back of a big grizzly bear!

Poetic Practice

"Annabella Stout" is a poem with eight characters. Each one has a different way of speaking — whining or groaning, mumbling or moaning. How does the character you're playing feel? Find the emotion and deliver your line.

This is great fun to do with a group of friends. Share the parts — doubling or tripling up the roles, if necessary.

Annabella Stout

by Deborah Dunleavy

Annabella Stout loved to shout.
Mr. McFellow would clearly bellow.
Dinah Divine would constantly whine,
And Peter Stimper could only whimper.
Mrs. Wumble would mumble and grumble,
And Greta Gabble had the gift of babble.
Poor Rebecca Roan would moan and groan,
But let us not forget Ms. Piggle —
Everyone loved to hear her giggle.

Sing Your Lines

For more character practice, try singing "Annabella Stout" in these different singing styles:

- the world's greatest opera star
- a heavy metal singer
- a serenading cowpoke
- a cool rap maestro

RT Tip Sheet 1: Reading

So how do you get an audience to hang on your every word? Here are a few professional tips.

Hold On

- Don't strangle the script. Hold it in one hand by the top, bottom or spine.
- You can use your script as a prop, especially if the story calls for a fly buzzing around your head.
- You can also set the script on a music stand or lectern and use both hands for gestures.

Chin Up

- You have to look at your script to read the words, but don't bury your head in it. Keep your chin up!
- Look away from your script to deliver some of your lines. Focus your eyes on a spot on the wall above the audience.

Don't Look

- Players never look at each other when they're performing.
- When you're not reading, look straight ahead.

Words Out Loud

Are you getting your bearings yet? Here are two silly scripts to read to practice your RT tips.

How to Train a Flea

You can train a pet flea to walk a tightrope, jump through hoops and swing on a trapeze. Follow these three simple steps.

STEP 1: Choose the most muscular flea at your local flea store. Strength is critical.

STEP 2: Never shout when training your flea. They have sensitive ears and delicate feelings.

STEP 3: Always reward your flea with a nice fresh peach at the end of every practice. In no time at all, you will be ready to join the flea circus when it comes to town.

How to Get to Timbuktu

Getting to Timbuktu is as easy as getting to the moon, or so they say. So what's the problem? No imagination? First, you must seek out the highest being — which is the sun. If it is a cloudy day, then you're out of luck. You might as well bury your head in the sand! Suppose it's a sunny day. Follow your shadow until you bump into something. If it is a wall, go over it. If it is a mailbox, put a stamp on your forehead and climb inside. If it is a police officer, ask directions. Next, look for a rubber dinghy and hope you are at the seashore. Paddle until the next full moon. By then you should be at Timbuktu or the moon or stuck in the middle of the ocean — wishing you had never started this silly thing in the first place. Good luck!

RT Tip Sheet 2: Scripting

Legends, poems and newspaper stories — you can turn anything you love to read into Readers' Theater. Here are some tips to help you turn a favorite read into a read-aloud script.

Dialogue

- Look for dialogue — the talk between two characters.
- You can leave out things like "he said" or "the snake hissed" when creating your script. If you leave them in the script, the whole line is read in the character's voice.

Narration

- Narration tells the audience what is happening. It fills in important details about who, what, where and how.
  - Sometimes one person reads the narration. Sometimes several readers take turns. When two or more people read the narration together like a chorus of voices, the story gets more dramatic.

Script

- Each player needs a copy of the script. Put each script in a binder that can be folded over and held in one hand or placed on a music stand or lectern.
- On your copy of the script, highlight everything you say and underline any movement or gestures you need to make.

This Street
by Deborah Dunleavy

EVERYONE: This street is an alphabet of stores.

READER 1: Appliance rentals and art supplies.

READER 2: Beauty salons — every description and size.

READER 3: A candy shop.

READER 4: And comics, too.

EVERYONE: A dance studio at No. 22.

READER 1: Electronic devices.

READER 2: Flowers that bloom.

READER 3: A garage.

READER 4: A hat shop.

READERS 3 AND 4: An ice-cream room.

READER 2: Jewelry for the hand and ear.

READER 1: A junk place right over here.

READER 3: Kites that fly. Laundry that spins.

READER 4: A music shop with CD bins.

READER 1: A newspaper stand by the optometrist's door.

READER 2: A pet shop where cats meow and roar.

EVERYONE: What's your question? There are no Qs for sale — that's our confession!

READER 3: There's a refrigerator repair.

READER 4: A shoe repair. A TV repair and an upholsterer.

READER 3: That's a chair repair.

READER 1: There's a video store.

READER 2: Watches to buy and sell.

EVERYONE: X!

READER 3: I'm X-hausted!

READER 4: This street is an alphabet of stores.

READERS 1, 2 AND 4: And around the block are a whole lot more.

READER 3: Thank goodness, I've come to Zed. Too many stores for my weary head!

OR

READER 3: Thank goodness, I've come to Zee. Enough stores for this ___ spree!

Streetscape Script

Take your audience on a guided tour of this busy street. In this script, there are four readers, and they all join in to play the part of "Everyone." You can change this poem into a script for two readers, or get your whole class to do it.

~~~~~~

This Street
by Deborah Dunleavy

EVERYONE: This street is an alphabet of stores.

READER 1: Appliance rentals and art supplies.

READER 2: Beauty salons — every description and size.

READER 3: A candy shop.

READER 4: And comics, too.

EVERYONE: A dance studio at No. 22.

READER 1: Electronic devices.

READER 2: Flowers that bloom.

READER 3: A garage.

READER 4: A hat shop.

READERS 3 AND 4: An ice-cream room.

READER 2: Jewelry for the hand and ear.

READER 1: A junk place right over here.

READER 3: Kites that fly. Laundry that spins.

READER 4: A music shop with CD bins.

READER 1: A newspaper stand by the optometrist's door.

READER 2: A pet shop where cats meow and roar.

EVERYONE: What's your question? There are no Qs for sale — that's our confession!

READER 3: There's a refrigerator repair.

READER 4: A shoe repair. A TV repair and an upholsterer.

READER 3: That's a chair repair.

READER 1: There's a video store.

READER 2: Watches to buy and sell.

EVERYONE: X!

READER 3: I'm X-hausted!

READER 4: This street is an alphabet of stores.

READERS 1, 2 AND 4: And around the block are a whole lot more.

READER 3: Thank goodness, I've come to Zed. Too many stores for my weary head!

OR

READER 3: Thank goodness, I've come to Zee. Enough stores for this shopping spree!

RT Tip Sheet 3: Staging

Remember the rule of thumb: Keep it simple!

Costumes

- Players dress in black turtlenecks and pants. Or the whole cast wears simple tunics or plain T-shirts.

Stage and Set

- The audience is usually in front of the readers, but try seating them on three sides — as if around a thrust stage.
- Set chair-height stools in a line or semi-circle. Or set up cubes so that some readers stand and others sit.
- A portable screen makes a simple backdrop.

Positions

- Readers are in position on stage when the audience arrives. Or they enter and go to their places after everyone is seated.
- Readers do not move around on the stage. You can use gestures, but only from the position you're already in.
- At the end, readers turn their backs to the audience or exit to one side of the stage.

Bolt of Lightning Strikes the *J.B. King*

This true story happened on June 26, 1930, on the St. Lawrence River near Brockville, Ontario. A bolt of lightning struck a drilling barge, called the *J.B. King*, and the ship exploded. There was a crew of 42 men; 30 died. This script comes word for word from a report in the *Brockville Recorder and Times*.

There are six readers: three narrators and three characters. The readers start with their backs to the audience and turn around just before speaking.

READER 1: *(Turns to the audience.)* Nature lifts its mighty hand, and in one swift sweep, deals a terrific blow.

READER 2: *(Turns to the audience.)* One minute the *King* was in plain sight, the next minute it disappeared.

READER 3: *(Turns to the audience.)* No bodies.

READER 1: Depth and swiftness of water make divers' work perilous.

READER 2: Body of Christopher Peterson found floating — 28 missing.

READER 3: Thirty lives are taken.

READER 1: One of the few persons to see the terrible explosion was a woman, Mrs. R.H. Wickens …

READER 2: … who resides at a summer cottage at Fernbank …

READER 3: … directly across from the spot where the tragedy occurred …

EVERYONE: … and less than a mile from the shoal on which the ill-fated vessel was working.

(Readers turn their backs to the audience and exit. Characters enter.)

MRS. WICKENS: With Mrs. Clark *(gestures to one side)* and Mrs. McNeil *(gestures to the other side)*, I was sitting on the porch of the Clark cottage.

MRS. CLARK: We knew that the dredge was ready …

MRS. MCNEIL: … or nearly so …

MRS. WICKENS: … nearly so, to "shoot" the holes which had been drilled.

MRS. CLARK: Mrs. McNeil had been picnicking with her five children …

MRS. WICKENS: … but when it started to rain heavily she rowed over for shelter.

MRS. MCNEIL: Well, we just sat there, talking, you know, with no thought of what was to come.

MRS. CLARK: We could see the boat quite plainly over on the shore of Cockburn Island.

MRS. WICKENS: Then quite suddenly, the *King* was obscured by a heavy blanket of smoke.

MRS. MCNEIL: I didn't think anything of it at all.

MRS. CLARK: Just figured they were blasting again.

MRS. WICKENS: There was a fairly heavy report …

MRS. CLARK: … but not as loud as it has been.

MRS. MCNEIL: I couldn't understand it.

MRS. WICKENS: And unlike ordinary blasts, this time there were two — one right after the other.

MRS. CLARK: It was ghastly.

MRS. MCNEIL: One minute that boat was right there, in plain sight.

EVERYONE: And then it was gone.

Story Theater

Take RT one step further and turn it into ST — Story Theater.
It's like Readers' Theater, but with costumes, props and action.

Rabbit and the Moon

A folk tale adapted by Deborah Dunleavy
Get creative with this script. Wear masks. Move around the
stage. Include a mime who mimes the actions of the characters.

This Khoikhoi folk tale from southern Africa explains two
things: why people die and why the rabbit has a split in its nose.

NARRATOR: The moon had a very important message to send
to Man. So she called forth an insect.

MOON: Tell Man that as I, the moon, live and dying live, so
shall Man live and dying live. Do you understand?

INSECT: Yes, I do understand. As you, the moon,
live and dying live, so shall Man live and dying live.

MOON: Very well. Be on your way.

NARRATOR: The insect had not gone very far when all of a sudden a rabbit jumped in front of it.

RABBIT: Where are you going?

INSECT: I'm on my way to Man.

RABBIT: On your way to Man? What for?

INSECT: I have a very important message to take to Man from the moon.

RABBIT: Is that right? Well, why don't you tell it to me? I have such big, strong legs, and I can get there a whole lot faster than a tiny insect.

INSECT: All right. But it is very important.

RABBIT: Tell me, tell me.

INSECT: The moon says that, as she lives and dying lives, so shall Man live and dying live.

RABBIT: No problem.

NARRATOR: And, just like that, the rabbit took off in search of Man. Finally, he saw a farmer.

RABBIT: Yoo-hoo! Man. It's me, the rabbit. I have a very important message for you from the moon.

FARMER: Really? Well then, speak up.

RABBIT: Moon says that as … *(Pause.)*

FARMER: Yes?

RABBIT: Moon says that as she … *(Pause.)*

FARMER: Go on.

RABBIT: Moon says that, as she lives and dying lives, your life will soon be over.

NARRATOR: Man was so sad to hear that his life would soon come to an end that, as he walked away, a tear fell down his cheek. But the rabbit thought that he had done the right thing, so he went hopping all the way back to the moon.

RABBIT: Moon. Moon. It's me, the rabbit. I took your message to Man.

MOON: My message to Man? I gave no message to a rabbit. I gave a message to an insect. What did you tell Man?

RABBIT: I just said that as you, the Moon, live and dying live, Man's life will soon be over.

NARRATOR: Moon was so upset with the rabbit that she picked up a stick and tapped it right on the end of its nose.

EVERYONE: And that is why rabbits have little splits in their noses.

RADIO PLAYS

Welcome to the weird and wonderful world of radio! In radio drama, you'll be using your voice, music and sound effects to create some amazing "theater of the mind."

- Sound like a traffic jam or a herd of horses.
- Invent wacky radio commercials.
- Perform a radio play starring King Arthur and Merlin.

Theater of the Mind

Radio drama is often called "theater of the mind." That's because radio plays come alive, not on a real stage, but in the minds of the audience. Listeners have to imagine what the play's characters, setting and action look like.

War of the Worlds

War of the Worlds — one of the scariest radio dramas of all time — was broadcast on the night before Halloween in 1938. People who tuned in at the beginning of the program knew that they were listening to a play that radio actor Orson Welles had adapted from a short story by H.G. Wells. But listeners who tuned in late really believed that Martians were invading New York City. There was mass panic as thousands of people hid in their cellars or ran into the streets to escape the aliens.

The Golden Age of Radio

The 1930s and 1940s were the golden age of radio — when families huddled around their radio sets to catch the latest episode of their favorite shows or the latest news flash about the war.

The Lone Ranger

For the first time in 1933, families tuned in and heard those famous words "Hi-Ho, Silver! A fiery horse with the speed of light — A cloud of dust — And a hearty Hi-Ho Silver! The Lone Ranger!"

The Adventures of Superman

Superman started as a comic-book character in 1938. In 1940, he hit the radio airwaves — "It's a bird! It's a plane! It's Superman!"

Radio Voices

To stage a radio play, you need three things: voices, sound effects and music. Most important are the voices. They set the scene, tell the story and express mood and emotion.

Voice Gymnastics

How versatile and acrobatic are your vocal cords? Develop your radio voice by trying out these voice warm-ups.

Warm-Up 1: Volume

Read the sentence below five times. Each time change the volume of your voice. Start off really loud, and then get gradually quieter until you're whispering. Notice how changing your volume changes the mood of the line.

That is the most beautiful hat I have ever seen.

Warm-Up 2: Tempo

Read the line below five times. Each time change the tempo of your voice. Start off saying the sentence really fast, and then gradually slow down.

Oh, my goodness, look at that!

Warm-Up 3: Pitch

Pitch is about how high or low you can make your voice. Try the sentence below first in a high voice, then gradually send your voice lower.

I really want an ice-cream cone.

You can also change your pitch in mid-sentence. Try the sentence below, starting high and ending low. Then say it again starting low and ending high. Notice how the meaning changes.

Do you want to see a movie?

Warm-Up 4: Stress

Which word is the most important word? When you put stress or emphasis on a particular word, the sentence takes on a whole different meaning. Try this:

What am I doing?

What **am** I doing?

What am **I** doing?

What am I **doing**?

123

How Do You Feel?

Sad, frustrated, bored, upset, scared? Your voice will tell listeners how your character feels and what is about to happen in your radio play. Practice saying these lines using different emotions. Notice how different emotions create different attitudes.

Happy/Sad

The little boy noticed an old woman sitting beside the road.

Excited/Curious

The trumpets roared! The drums rolled! The people cheered!

Angry/Afraid

One day, all the animals set out for the deepest part of the jungle.

Tale Spins

Think about these questions and create a short tale — full of emotion and attitude.

- What did the old woman say to the little boy?
- Who was leading the animals into the jungle?
- What were the people cheering about?

124

The True Story

Suppose you were really there when Humpty Dumpty fell from the wall. Here's a chance to tell your side of the story.

Your Story

First, get your story straight!

Who are you?
The queen? A soldier in the king's army?
One of the king's horses? A servant?

What were you doing when Humpty fell?
Sipping tea? Practicing your jousting?
Cleaning the stable?

When did all this happen?
First thing in the morning? At lunchtime?
At sunset?

How did it happen?
Was Humpty just being clumsy?
Did someone push him?

What did you do?
Help him? Scold him? Laugh?

The Cook's Story

Here's one version of the story. Read it in your best cook's voice.

So there I was — baking tarts for the queen. I was just putting them on the window ledge to cool, when I saw it. I saw everything! Humpty was pushed, I tell you! Three stable boys danced around him, calling him names. One threw a stone at him. And then another just pushed poor Humpty right off the wall. It was terrible, I tell you! Just terrible! I told the queen right away, I did.

Sound Effects

Sound effects are used for two things in radio plays. Background sounds — such as waves or thunder — set the play's scene and mood. Other sounds — such as creaking doors or galloping horses — imitate action in the play.

You can makc all sorts of sound effects using your voice, body, real objects and musical instruments. Try some of these.

Thunder

Shake or wobble a cookie sheet.

Fire

Crumple up a cellophane bag or newspaper.

Crickets

Rub a finger along the teeth of a comb.

Horses' Hooves

Clap two empty plastic containers together with a galloping rhythm.

Rain

Sprinkle salt into a cone of wax paper.

Waves

Swish popcorn from side to side in a large plastic bowl.

Walking

Fill a cookie sheet with gravel and walk on it.

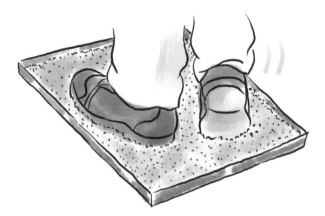

Recorded Sounds

You can record some sounds for your play — an alarm clock, a doorbell, a telephone ringing, an old-fashioned typewriter, traffic at a busy street corner, background voices.

Keyboard Sounds

With a keyboard you can invent sounds. You can record your budgie chirping, and then change the pitch and length of the sound to make it really strange. If you connect your keyboard to a computer, you can store these sounds.

Music

Strike a drum, ring a bell, pluck a string. These sounds can change the mood of your radio play. If you rub a guitar pick up and down a heavy metal guitar string, you'll get a sound like a creaky door.

Do-It-Yourself Haunted House

Here's a radio play full of sound effects. One player reads the story and pauses after each set of bold words so the other players can make the sound effects.

Haunted House on the Hill

It was a dark and gloomy night. **The wind was howling.** I decided that this was the perfect night to visit the haunted house on the hill. **It started to rain.** A bolt of lightning flashed through the sky. **Thunder roared.** Just then **an owl screeched.** Shivers ran up and down my spine.

I walked down the pathway, and then **climbed up the old wooden steps** to the front door. Slowly, **I opened the door.** A bunch of **bats flew out. The door slammed shut.**

Everything was black. **I tried the light switch,** but it didn't work. So I used my flashlight. I thought I could hear a **witch cackling.** It was getting **louder and louder.** Something jumped out at me. It was only **a cat.**

I heard terrible sounds coming from the closet at the end of the hallway. Someone was **moaning and groaning. I tiptoed up to the door.** It had to be a ghost. I opened the door. It was nothing but **a cricket.**

Upstairs I could hear **footsteps.** Not normal footsteps. These were **big footsteps.** They were **huge.** I turned around and **ran as fast as I could.** I stopped at the doorway to catch my breath. I was leaning against a cuckoo clock. It was striking — **eleven, twelve, thirteen.**

Then Mom called from downstairs: **"Breakfast!" I yawned.** That was some nightmare!

Wacky Commercials

Imagine a new and amazing invention. Make up a commercial using voice, music and sound effects. Try this one first.

Sneakos: The Invisible Sneakers

Theme music: *A favorite song. Fade in. Play for a few seconds. Fade out.*

Sound effect: *Laughter fades in, then out to the sound of footsteps. A door opens and closes.*

ALEX: I'm home.

ANNOUNCER: When you get home from school and your parent says …

PARENT: Put your shoes away. I'm tired of tripping over them.

ANNOUNCER: It's time to reach for amazing Sneakos. Just push the red button on the heel and — zippo — your shoes are out of sight and out of mind.

ALEX: No problem, out of sight, out of mind.

ANNOUNCER: To find your Sneakos, clap three times, and they will appear like magic before your very eyes.

Sound effect: *Three claps.*

ALEX: (*excited*) All right!

PARENT: Don't forget your homework.

ALEX: (*disappointed*) Okay.

Sound effect: *Footsteps.*

ALEX: Wish somebody would invent homework that gets done on its own.

ANNOUNCER: Step into Sneakos — the amazing invisible shoe.

Theme music: *Fade in and out.*

Merlin and King Arthur

What if Merlin were alive today and you could ask him to tell you all about King Arthur?

Cast of Characters

- Merlin
- Two children
- Three knights
- Sir Kay
- King Arthur
- Sir Ector
- Onlooker

Music

- Recorder playing "Early One Morning."

Sound Effects

- Snoring
- Alarm clock ringing
- Trumpet fanfare
- Whirling-wind time-travel sound
- Footsteps
- Clanging cans for knights in suits of armor
- Galloping horses
- Murmuring voices
- Cheering voices

Music cue: "Early One Morning."

Sound effect: Snoring.

Sound effect: Alarm clock ringing.

MERLIN: Who woke me up?

CHILDREN: We did. We did. It's show time.

MERLIN: Ah, yes, I have a story to tell. My name is Merlin and I am a …

(He forgets because he is old and sleepy.)

FIRST CHILD: A wizard.

SECOND CHILD: A magician.

MERLIN: Yes, I am a magician and a wizard. I have lived in the past and I see into the future. I have stood beside the Knights of the Round Table. I have fought fire-breathing dragons. I have …

FIRST CHILD: Merlin, tell us about Arthur.

SECOND CHILD: King Arthur.

MERLIN: Very well, then — the story of Arthur Pendragon.

Sound effect: Trumpet.

MERLIN: Long ago …

CHILDREN: How long ago?

MERLIN: Before you were born. Now shall I tell the story? *(Pause.)* Long ago, in the land of enchanted forests, there was a mighty king.

CHILDREN: King Arthur!

MERLIN: No! Uther Pendragon. Now do I have to turn you into mice or will you listen?

CHILDREN: We're listening.

MERLIN: Uther ruled over Britain until he died. Everybody and his uncle wanted to take over the kingdom. Even his stepdaughter, Morgan LeFay, tried to claim the throne. Things were a real mess so somebody had to do something. That was the Christmas I stuck the sword in the stone.

Sound effect: Time-travel whirling-wind sound.

Sound effect: Footsteps.

MERLIN: I place this sword within this stone,
Let all come claim King Uther's throne.
But only one shall pull it free,
And king of Britain shall he be.

Sound effect: Clanging suits of armor.

FIRST KNIGHT: I am the bravest knight in the land. Let me try. (*Groan. Puff. Pant.*) Grrrr …

FIRST CHILD: I think it's stuck, sir.

Sound effect: Galloping horses and clanging suits of armor.

SECOND KNIGHT: Surely I can pull it out. (*Grunt. Groan.*)

Sound effect: Clanging suits of armour.

THIRD KNIGHT: Out of the way. It's my turn. (*Grunt. Groan.*)

MERLIN: No one could pull the sword out of the stone. Then one day Sir Ector brought his two sons, Sir Kay and Arthur, to a tournament.

Sound effect: Trumpet fanfare and cheering crowd.

SIR KAY: Oh drat! I forgot my sword. Arthur, what can I do?

MERLIN: Sir Kay was very forgetful. Arthur was very kind.

ARTHUR: I will run home and get your sword for you.

MERLIN: When Arthur got home, he found the door locked. Suddenly, Arthur remembered that he had seen a sword sticking out of a stone at the side of the road. So he went to that very place and pulled the sword out. Arthur did not know about Merlin's spell. But Sir Kay did. He took the sword and went to show his father.

SIR KAY: Look, Father. I have the sword from the stone. I must be the rightful king!

SIR ECTOR: Show me how you did this, my son.

SIR KAY: Well, I … it was Arthur who, well, umm …

MERLIN: Arthur spoke up.

ARTHUR: Give me the sword, and I will put it back. There, it is in the stone again.

CHILDREN: What happened? What happened?

MERLIN: Try as they might with all their might, neither Sir Kay nor Sir Ector could pull out the sword. Soon a crowd gathered around them.

Sound effect: Many footsteps and murmuring voices.

ONLOOKER: Let young Arthur try!

MERLIN: No one spoke a word. Arthur reached down and pulled the sword out of the stone.

Sound effect: Cheers: "Arthur is king! Long live the king!"

FIRST CHILD: And that's what really happened?

MERLIN: As I stand before you now, I stood beside Arthur then. But there is something I haven't told you. Arthur was really King Uther's son.

SECOND CHILD: No kidding?

MERLIN: I took Arthur to Sir Ector when he was just a baby so he would be kept safe until he was old enough to become king. And so Arthur became king at the age of 16. (*Pause.*) Now can I go back to sleep?

Sound effect: Recorder music and snoring.

ACT III: GETTING YOUR ACT TOGETHER

In Act III, you'll be putting your voice and body together to create some amazing characters and magical stories. This section is full of improvisation games that will give your imagination a good workout. Get set to explore all the dramatic ups and downs of ...

- Melodrama
- Comedy
- Tragedy

135

MELODRAMA

Do you like bigger-than-life heroes and villains? Stories that keep you on the edge of your seat? Happy endings? That's melodrama!

- Play the villain everybody loves to hate.
- Take the actor's "hot seat."
- Create your own melodrama.

Pot-Boilers and Tear-Jerkers

If you could step into a time machine and go to an English theater in the 1800s, you'd probably end up watching a melodrama. Audiences loved these pot-boilers and tear-jerkers — stories full of good guys, bad guys, beautiful maidens and cliff-hanger endings. People in the audience would boo and hiss at the villain and cry over the fate of the heroine.

Melodramatic Characters

There's nothing complicated about the characters in a melodrama. They are either very, very good or very, very bad — like characters in adventure comics or fairy tales. There is always a creepy villain (the bad character), a brave hero (the good character) and usually a fair maiden.

Melodramatic Plots

Plot involves the action in a play — what the characters do. In all plays, there is a conflict or problem that has to be fixed or solved. In melodrama, the villain is always up to no good and the hero always saves the day — and sometimes wins the love of the fair maiden. In the end, good always triumphs over evil, and everyone (except the villain, of course) lives happily ever after.

The characters and plots in melodrama appeal to our strong emotions. As the plot unfolds, we get to hiss at the villain and cheer on the hero. That's what makes melodrama so much fun!

MUSICAL MELODRAMA

The word "melodrama" comes from Greek. "Melos" means "song." In ancient Greek melodrama, in opera and in nineteenth-century melodrama, music was played to boost the emotions of the audience.

You Must Pay the Rent!

Here's a mini-melodrama script to try. You play all three characters. Use your finger as the bow in the hair of the maiden, as a bow tie for the brave hero and as a mustache for the nasty villain.

VILLAIN: You must pay the rent!

MAIDEN: I can't pay the rent.

VILLAIN: You must pay the rent.

MAIDEN: I can't pay the rent.

VILLAIN: You must pay the rent or ...

HERO: I'll pay the rent.

MAIDEN: My hero!

VILLAIN: Curses, foiled again!

You Must Eat Your Spinach!

Melodramas sometimes happen at home! Does this one sound familiar?

MOTHER: You must eat your spinach.

CHILD: I don't want to eat my spinach.

FATHER: You must eat your spinach.

CHILD: I don't want to eat my spinach.

MOTHER AND FATHER: You must eat your spinach or no TV tonight!

SUPERMAN: I'll eat the spinach.

CHILD: It's a bird? It's a plane? No! It's Superman!

SUPERMAN: You got it kid. Check out the muscles. I always eat my spinach.

CHILD: Me, too!

Your Turn!

Make up a melodramatic scene with these lines. Then try some of your own ideas.

- You must walk the dog!
- You must take out the garbage!
- You must do your homework!

Snapshots

One way you can tell who's who in a melodrama is by the way a character moves. A creepy villain, for example, might slink around checking over his shoulder. Don't forget to make your movements bigger than life.

Everybody Freeze!

In this game, everybody gets to walk in the shoes of the villain, hero and maiden — before freezing on the spot. The players can take turns being the leader.

- Everyone walks around — normal style.
- Leader calls "Villain!"
- Everyone walks like a villain.
- Leader calls "Snapshot!"
- Everyone freezes as the villain.
- Repeat for the hero and the maiden.

To the Dragon's Cave

The villain has kidnapped the maiden and is taking her to the dragon's cave. The hero is in hot pursuit! What happens when they meet the dragon? Does the dragon scold the villain? Maybe the dragon falls in love with the maiden and makes the hero cry!

Create your own plot and act it out. Without any warning, the player who is the leader calls "Snapshot!" Everybody freezes — creating a frozen picture of your melodrama.

Slide Show

When you put a series of snapshots together, you end up with a slide show. Silently act out "You Must Pay the Rent" in a series of four frozen snapshots. If you have more than three people in your group, some can be the audience, who show in their faces and bodies how they feel about the situation. Other players can have fun being the furniture in the play.

Silent Flick

Have you ever watched an old silent movie? Everything seems to happen in jerky motions. You can turn one of your melodramas into a silent movie by using a strobe light.

Silently and in slow motion, act out "You Must Pay the Rent" or one of your own melodramas. Turn off all the lights, and turn on a flickering strobe. Play exciting music that rises and falls with the action. Or ask your audience to hum a movie song that everybody knows.

Princess to the Rescue!

In melodramas in the old days, the villains were always men and so were the heroes. Thank goodness, those days are over!

Create your own scene for a melodrama, but make the hero character a girl, the rescued character a boy and the villain a "she" rather than a "he." Then play the snapshot game. How would a heroic girl move? A villainous "she"? Here's a script to try for starters.

Boy Soup

SHE VILLAIN: Just what I was looking for — a boy to flavor my soup!

BOY: Please, please! Don't put me in the pot!

SHE VILLAIN: Yum, yum. How tasty you'll be!

BOY: Please! Don't cook me in the pot!

SHE VILLAIN: Ha! Ha! Your time has come …

GIRL HERO: Stop right there! He's spoiled rotten. He'll only ruin your soup.

Fractured Fairy Tale

Fairy tales are stories we all know and love. A fractured fairy tale is a familiar story with a funny new twist.

Create a melodrama by fracturing your favorite fairy tale. What happens if Cinderella doesn't like the Prince? What if the mirror breaks every time Snow White looks at herself? What if the troll in "The Three Billy Goats Gruff" is really a good guy?

Here is a fractured fairy tale to try.

The Wolf and the Pigs

FIRST PIG: Oh no! Here comes the wolf.

WOLF: (*Singing a happy tune.*) Merrily, we roll along, roll along …

SECOND PIG: Egads! Don't let him in.

WOLF: (*In a sweet voice.*) Hallooo! Is anybody home?

THIRD PIG: He's going to huff and puff and blow our house down!

WOLF: I've brought you a fresh apple pie.

PIGS: We love apple pie!

NARRATOR: And so the wolf and the pigs dined on fresh apple pie and made plans for a Sunday picnic.

Hot Seat!

In this game, one player sits on a chair — the hot seat — playing the part of a character in a melodrama. The other players get to ask the character questions. What questions would you ask the villain, hero and maiden in "You Must Pay the Rent"? Or the wicked stepmother in "Snow White"? Or the poor troll who wants to be a good guy in a fractured version of "The Three Billy Goats Gruff"?

Now, Mr. Wolf, what exactly did you have for dinner last night?

Melodramatic Monologue

Have some fun making up a heroic or villainous monologue. A monologue is one actor speaking aloud to herself or himself, or to another actor or directly to the audience. Practice with "Jack's Monologue" and then try "Guess Who?".

Jack's Monologue

The giant was after me. I ran so fast I could hardly breathe. I headed straight to the beanstock. The giant was only a few feet behind. I hid behind a rock and felt the whole earth tremble as he rushed by. When the coast was clear, I jumped onto the vine and scrambled down. I looked up. The giant's feet were coming toward me through the clouds. That's when I shouted for my mother to bring me the ax.

Guess Who?

Pick a fairy-tale character and create a monologue. The tricky part is that you can't reveal who you are! Make your friends guess what character you're playing. Who do you think this character is?

Never! Never! She'll never guess my name! She might win a gold medal on the spinning wheel — but that won't help her now. Not in a million years! Ha! Ha! In three days' time, her child will be mine.

Answer: Rumpelstiltskin

A Thousand Times No!

Get out your hankies for a real tear-jerker. This melodrama comes from a song by Sherman, Lewis and Silver, published in 1934. There are three main characters: a fair maiden who loves to swoon and faint, a villain who sneaks around and a brave hero who comes to the rescue. The minor characters include the girl's mother and father and a minister for the wedding. The characters act out their parts while they recite the lyrics.

MAIDEN:
She was a child of the valley,
An innocent maiden was she;

VILLAIN:
He was desperate Desmond
Who owned all the town's property.

HERO:
He would pursue her through hills and through
    dells,
But she was wise to his game.
Each time he threatened,

VILLAIN:
You'll wed me or else,

PARENTS:
These are the words she'd exclaim:

MAIDEN:
No! No! A thousand times No!
You cannot buy my caress.
No! No! A thousand times No!
I'd rather die than say Yes.

MOTHER:
Ah, but this poisonous villain,
He wouldn't leave her alone. Said

VILLAIN:
Either join me in wedlock
Or I'll kick you out of your home.

MOTHER:
She knew her people so feeble and old
Needed a roof o'er their head,

FATHER:
Winter would soon bring the snow and
    the cold,
Yet she defied them and said:

MAIDEN:
No! No! A thousand times No!
You cannot buy my caress.
No! No! A thousand times No!
I'd rather die than say Yes.

148

VILLAIN:
That night he crept up to her window,
And oh! how that villain could creep!
He stole her out of her boudoir,
And kidnapped her while fast asleep.

FATHER:
He tied the gal to the old railroad track,

MOTHER:
The milk train was rushing downhill,
She cried to him,

MAIDEN:
Though my future looks black,
You buzzard, my answer is still:

ALL BUT THE VILLAIN:
No! No! A thousand times No!

MAIDEN:
You cannot buy my caress.

ALL BUT THE VILLAIN:
No! No! A thousand times No!

MAIDEN:
I'd rather die than say Yes.

FATHER:
Now she loved the young village blacksmith,

MOTHER:
A muscular "he" man was he,

HERO:
He heard that his love was in danger,
And right to the rescue flew he.
He grabbed his darling in "thee" nick of time
And yelled, "This is my future wife."

VILLAIN:
The villain sneered, "Blacksmith, that
maiden is mine."

HERO:
The hero cried, "Not on your life!
No! No! A thousand times No!
You cannot buy her caress.
No! No! A thousand times No!
She'd rather die than say Yes."

ALL BUT VILLAIN:
Now this is the end of our story,
Her honor was left without stain,

MINISTER:
The hero took her to the altar,

VILLAIN:
The villain was foiled once again.

PARENTS:
The mortgage was paid and the
handsome young swain
Moved in with her folks right away,

MAIDEN AND HERO:
Their life is contented though simple and
plain,
And no more will she have to say:

ALL BUT HERO:
No! No! A thousand times No!
You cannot buy my caress.
No! No! A thousand times No!
I'd rather die than say Yes.

COMEDY

Get set to tickle some funny bones! There's every sort of comedy to try and comedians to play. Have fun with your friends doing alphabet improv, knock-knock jokes and some one-liners from Shakespeare.

- Act out a joke.
- Do stand-up comedy.
- Put on a fool's play.

151

Comedy Old and New

Comedy is all about making people laugh, and people have been making other people laugh since one of our prehistoric ancestors first slipped on a banana peel.

Old Greek Comedy

In ancient Greece, people flocked to the theater to watch the comedies of Aristophanes. They were full of foolish stock characters, fantastic settings and silly situations that poked fun at the rules and rulers of Athens. His comedies featured a costumed chorus of 24 actors who commented on the action in the plays.

Shakespearean Comedy

No stock comic characters for William Shakespeare! The most famous playwright of all time peopled his plays with believable, lifelike characters. Even his fools — such as Feste and Bottom — have personalities with all the quirks of human nature. As in real life, the personalities of his comic characters change and develop as the plays progress.

Comedy High and Low

Some comedies make us fall down laughing. Some make us chortle and feel good when the plot ends happily. And some do both. It all depends on what kind of comedy we're watching!

Farce

If you're watching a Three Stooges movie or a Pink Panther movie, you're watching a kind of comedy called farce. It's full of zany humor, hilarious slapstick and ridiculous plots. This is sometimes called low comedy.

Situation Comedies

When we tune in the tube to our favorite sit-com, we're usually watching a mixture of high and low comedy. Many sit-coms have moments of farcical slapstick, but their humor is mostly about ordinary, down-to-earth characters working through a funny problem or situation that we can all identify with.

153

Gobbledygook Games

In comedy, a lot of humor depends on how you say things and how you act when you're saying them. Here are two games for two players that will help develop your comic voice and style.

Oogle Boogle

In this game, you try to get your partner to do something silly. You can only use gestures and made-up words, such as "gobbledygook."

- To start off, try to get your partner to jump up and down or move a chair.

Yes/No Game

In this partnership, one player can only say "yes," and the other can only say "no."

- You and your partner have just won the lottery. You have one week to claim your prize in a city that's very far away.

  Your partner wants to drive, but you're afraid of everything that travels on wheels. Try to convince your partner to walk all the way.

Knock, Knock!

A joke is just a joke. It is the way you tell it that makes it funny. This is a stand-up comedy routine for two or more players. Each player hides behind a large piece of bristol board decorated to look like a window or door. Keep the knock-knock jokes coming, one right after the other.

Remember: If the audience is laughing, pause and listen. How you look when you're listening can be funny, too.

Knock, knock.
Who's there?
Safari.
Safari who?
Safari so good.

Knock, knock.
Who's there?
Turnip.
Turnip who?
Turnip the volume,
I can't hear the
music.

Knock, knock.
Who's there?
Ben and Don.
Ben and Don who?
Ben there. Don that.

Knock, knock.
Who's there?
Gruesome.
Gruesome who?
Gruesome tomatoes
in my garden.

Comedy Team

One of the funniest stand-up teams of all time was Abbott and Costello. Bud Abbott, the "straight man," and Lou Costello, the funny man, started performing together on stage in the 1930s. Their most famous comedy routine is "Who's on First?" When Costello asks the names of the players on a baseball team, Abbott warns him that they all have very peculiar names: "Who's on first, What's on second, and I Don't Know's on third." What follows is a hilarious play on words as Costello gets frustrated trying to find out who's playing on first base and what's the name of the player on second base. Here's just a taste of their routine:

COSTELLO: What's the guy's name on first base?
ABBOTT: No, What's on second!
COSTELLO: I'm not asking you who's on second!
ABBOTT: Who's on first.
COSTELLO: I don't know.
ABBOTT: Oh, he's on third.

Team Routine

One of you delivers the straight lines and the other delivers the punch line. Try this routine, then create one of your own.

QUESTION: What do you call a carton full of ducks?
ANSWER: A box of quackers.
QUESTION: Why did the fool put his head on the piano?
ANSWER: He plays by ear.
QUESTION: How do you make a hot dog stand?
ANSWER: Take away its chair.

Act Out a Joke

Longer jokes can be acted out. This one calls for a knight, an innkeeper and a shaggy dog — and some fun sound effects.

A Shaggy Dog Joke

Sound effects: *Wind and rain. Horse's hooves.*

KNIGHT: What a stormy night! My horse is too tired to go on. Aha! Here is an inn.

(The knight walks to the door and knocks.)

INNKEEPER: I'm coming, I'm coming! Hold your horses.

Sound effects: *Creaky sound of the hinges of an old, heavy door.*

KNIGHT: Innkeeper, do you have a horse I can borrow?

INNKEEPER: I am sorry, sir. All I have is my dog.

(The dog rolls over, whines and barks.)

KNIGHT: Then I will ride the dog.

INNKEEPER: Are you kidding? I wouldn't send a knight out on a dog like this.

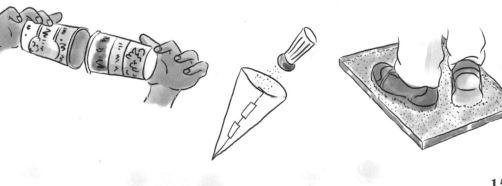

Improvisation

Acting out a scene without planning it is called improvisation — or improv, for short. There are no props, sets or scripts — you make everything up as you go along. Improv is quick, spontaneous and fun.

Three Bags Full

Here is a great improv game to play with your friends.

What You Need

Make "Who," "What" and "Where" bags. On strips of paper, write down some characters for the "Who Bag," activities for the "What Bag" and places for the "Where Bag." Here are some ideas.

WHO Bag
- baby
- rock star
- astronaut
- chef
- basketball player
- conductor

WHAT Bag
- mowing the lawn
- learning to roller-skate
- falling asleep
- watching a tennis match
- playing a violin
- eating spaghetti

WHERE Bag
- at the beach
- at a busy intersection
- on a farm
- at the zoo
- in an office
- at a supermarket

What You Do

Each player picks a who, a what and a where. This is a guessing game, so players need to keep everything secret. Each player gets 30 seconds to improvise before it's the audience's turn to guess who the player is playing, where the scene is set and what the activity is.

Here's an example to get you started. In this scene, an astronaut and chef fall asleep at the zoo.

ASTRONAUT: I always get that weightless feeling when I come here.

CHEF: (*Yawns.*) I feel like something to eat. Maybe I can make us a pizza.

ASTRONAUT: All this blasting off and orbiting is getting to me. (*Head starts to nod.*)

CHEF: (*Imitating a monkey waking up the astronaut.*) Look at those. I bet I could make them banana cake.

ASTRONAUT: Sure beats the freeze-dried stuff I have to eat. (*Reaches into his pocket.*) Maybe these guys will like it.

Alphabet Improv

The players decide on the who, what and where of a scene. The first player acts out a sentence that starts with the letter "A." The second player acts out a sentence that starts with the letter "B." Keep going until you end with the letter "Z." In this scene, two children get lost in the woods.

Actually, I think we should turn back now.

But we can't.

Creepy, this place is really creepy.

Don't move! I hear something.

Easy. Listen.

Forget it. It's just an owl.

Good. I'm cold. Let's build a fire.

Hope we have some matches.

I didn't bring any.

Just our luck.

…

Zipper! My zipper is stuck.

Get into Character

These improv games are a great way to give your comic characters some real personality!

Zany Talk Show

Two players pretend to be a TV host and guest. The host introduces the guest, asks four or five questions and thanks the guest for being on the show. Try on some of these quirky personalities, then make up some of your own.

- a jet pilot who teaches pigs to fly
- an inventor who makes sunglasses for fish
- a person who walks backward

Will's One-Liners

This improv game starts with a line from a play by William Shakespeare. Take a few minutes to create some comic characters and a story line. Then let the play begin!

- "A horse! A horse! My kingdom for a horse!" (*King Richard III*)
- "Tush! tush! Fear boys with bugs." (*The Taming of the Shrew*)
- "A very ancient and fish-like smell." (*The Tempest*)

Foolish Business

Fools were the only members of royal courts who could speak the truth without being beheaded! They were wise and witty and could sometimes tell fortunes. In Shakespeare's play *Twelfth Night*, Viola speaks of Feste the fool: "This fellow's wise enough to play the fool." Above all, fools made people laugh.

What Kind of Fool Am I?

It's your turn to be a fool. Walk like a fool. Talk like a fool. Act like a fool.

- A chicken has escaped from its coop. You decide to rescue it!

Foolish Wisdom

You are a fool who really believes that people should marry brooms. Try your foolish wisdom on a partner. Your partner asks questions to trick you into saying "no."

QUESTION: Is it hard to hold hands with a broom?
FOOL: Ever since I was swept off my feet, we just hug.

QUESTION: Does your broom talk?
FOOL: Broom is a very good listener — and never interrupts!

QUESTION: Is your broom good-looking?
FOOL: Who cares! Love is blind.

The Wise People of Gotham

Here's a comedy script that will have your audience roaring with laughter.

Cast of Characters

- The town crier
- Two women
- Old man
- A woodcutter
- The king
- The sheriff
- A horse
- A child
- Dobbin, the wise man
- Townsfolk
- Lovable Fool
- Nervous Fool

Setting

A village market in the time of long ago. Everyone is busy: some people are sweeping the cobblestones, some are polishing apples, some are carrying buckets of water, etc.

Situation

The greedy king is coming to the village, and the people are afraid he will take everything they own.

TOWN CRIER: Hear ye! Hear ye! The king is coming. Prepare for the king! (*Repeats.*)

FIRST WOMAN: No, not the king!

SECOND WOMAN: Last time he took all of my chickens.

OLD MAN: And he stole my cow.

(*Everyone gathers together.*)

WOODCUTTER: Let's chop down the trees in the woods and block the highway that leads into town.

ALL: Yes! Of course! Let's do it!

(*Everyone starts chopping down trees and piling heavy logs on the highway.*)

WOODCUTTER: Here comes the king! Quick! Hide!

(*Everyone scatters and hides. The king and sheriff enter, followed by the horse. The horse does a clippity-clop dance in front of the king. The king stares at the horse.*)

KING: I should never have given that horse dance lessons!

(*The horse exits, kicking up its heels.*)

(*The king does a doubletake.*)

KING: (*Looking around.*) What is going on here?

(*The child enters.*)

KING: Who chopped these trees down? Who dares to block my way?

CHILD: (*Bowing to the king.*) The people of Gotham, your majesty.

KING: Well, then, tell the people of Gotham that I shall, I shall, I shall … (*The sheriff whispers in his ear.*) I shall come with my sheriff … yes, I shall come — and have all of their noses cut off!

SHERIFF: Well done, sir.

CHILD: (*Grabs nose.*) Oh no, not our noses!

(*The king and sheriff exit. The child runs to the townsfolk, who have been listening.*)

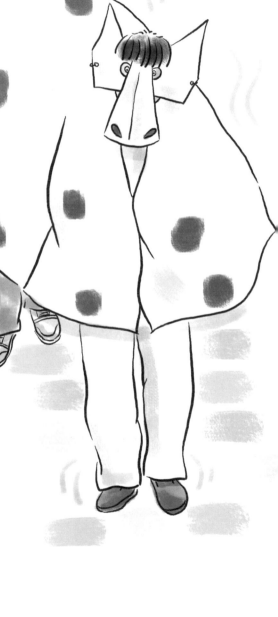

ALL: This is terrible, terrible. What shall we do? We must save our noses. We must save our noses. We must …

DOBBIN: We have been too wise, my friends, and look where it has got us. Often it is the wise who get punished, but I have never heard of anyone hurting a fool. When the king comes again, let us all act like fools.

ALL: Good! Good! We will act like fools.

(*Everyone does a silly walk. Some put on silly hats. Another dances with a broom. Another sits up like a dog. All the townspeople find something silly to do.*)

TOWN CRIER: Hear ye! Hear ye! The king is coming. Prepare for the king! (*Repeats.*)

(*The townspeople break into two groups — old people and young people. The old people start pushing huge boulders up a steep hill. The young people grunt very loudly.*)

KING: (*Turns to the old people.*) What are you doing?

OLD MAN: Rolling stones uphill to make the sun rise.

KING: You foolish fellow. Don't you know the sun will rise without your help?

OLD PEOPLE: Really!

OLD MAN: Well, I never thought of that. How wise you are!

(*The young people grunt and groan.*)

SHERIFF: (*Turns to the young people.*) And what — on earth — are you doing?

YOUNG PERSON: We are grunting while our parents do all the work.

SHERIFF: I see. I see. Let us move along, your majesty.

(*Some townspeople start building a wall. The king and sheriff move toward them.*)

KING: (*Turns to the townspeople.*) And what — pray tell — are you doing?

LOVABLE FOOL: (*Bows and then does a curtsey.*) Oh sir, don't you know? There is a cuckoo in this field. We are building a wall to keep it from wandering away, sir.

KING: You foolish people. Don't you know that the bird will simply fly over the wall no matter how high you build it?

LOVABLE FOOL: My goodness, sir. We never thought of that. How very wise you are, sir.

(*Nervous Fool enters. He is carrying a door on his back.*)

SHERIFF: And you — dare I ask? What are you doing?

NERVOUS FOOL: I am going on a long journey, my lord.

SHERIFF: But why are you carrying a door on your back?

NERVOUS FOOL: I left my money at home, my lord.

SHERIFF: But why did you not leave your door at home, too?

NERVOUS FOOL: It's simple, my lord. If I take my door with me, thieves can't break it down and steal my money.

SHERIFF: You foolish fellow! Leave the door at home and take the money with you.

NERVOUS FOOL: Oh my, my lord! I never thought of that. How very wise you are, my lord.

KING: I do believe this town is full of fools.

SHERIFF: It would be a shame to harm such simple people.

KING: Let us leave them with their noses and ride back to the castle. They are too silly to punish.

(*The king and sheriff march away. The townspeople march behind them. The king and sheriff stop. The townspeople suddenly start doing something silly. The king and sheriff look puzzled. They turn again and exit. The townspeople follow them.*)

ALL: The king is gone! The king is gone! Long live our noses!

TRAGEDY

"Double, double, toil and trouble." Be forewarned. Be prepared.
Be careful. Ahead lies the sad and serious business of tragedy!

- Make a family tableau.
- Write a tragedy.
- Perform a scene from Shakespeare.

A Very Sad Story

If Mr. Nice Guy slips on a banana peel, dusts himself off and goes on his merry way — that's comedy. But if Mr. Nice Guy slips on a banana peel, tumbles down a cliff, breaks his neck and dies — that's tragedy.

A tragedy is a play with a sad story to tell.

Some comedies have serious moments, and some tragedies have flashes of humor. But a comedy always ends happily, and a tragedy ends with pain and suffering. In all of Shakespeare's great tragedies — *Romeo and Juliet*, *Hamlet*, *Othello*, *King Lear*, *Antony and Cleopatra* and *Macbeth* — the main characters die in the end.

The tragic hero is a good person gone wrong.

When we watch a melodrama, we cheer when the villain is punished in the end. Villains are rotten to the core so we feel they deserve what they get. Not so with the tragic hero.

As the curtain closes on a tragedy, we're overwhelmed by feelings of pity and grief for the tragic hero. That's because the hero is basically a good person who takes a wrong turn. But a hero's fate is not a matter of bad luck. Tragic heroes are responsible for their downfall because of choices they make and actions they follow.

BACKUP CHORUS

The tragedies of ancient Greece always had a chorus — a group of actors who stood in the orchestra space of the amphitheater chanting and singing. The chorus was a very important part of Greek tragedy. These choral actors asked questions and offered advice. They reacted to the events going on in the play and gave the audience a chance to think about what was happening. Sometimes they sang and danced.

Believable Characters

Good tragedy depends on believable characters. To help develop a tragic character, imagine what your character looks like, sounds like and walks like.

Seeing Is Believing

If you can see the character in your mind, it's much easier to make your character come to life.

- Are you tall, short, stocky or thin?
- Do you have red hair, messy hair or no hair?
- Are you wearing old, worn-out clothes or expensive, new ones?

Talk On

Is your character's voice soft or rough, screechy or sweet? Find your voice with this tongue twister.

There's no need to light a night light
On a light night like tonight;
For a night light's a slight light
On a bright night like tonight.

Walk On

Two players walk in from opposite sides of the stage. One is stooped over and gloomy. The other is energetic and lively. They disappear behind a screen. The players reappear, but they have swapped characters.

Life Stories

Get to know your character better by inventing a biography. Where were you born? How old are you? What's your family like? Here's a game for a group of players that helps get to the heart of your life stories.

Family Tableau

Pretend you're having a family portrait painted. Strike a pose that shows what all the family members are really like. Stay as still as possible and don't speak. In drama, this is called a tableau. Try some of these family gatherings.

- A family dinner at great-great-great Uncle Ham's farmhouse.
- A royal family reunion in the Middle Ages.
- A family get-together on the moon.

Learning Your Lines

When you're learning your lines for a play, you'll discover that there is more than one way to deliver them. Trying different movements, gestures or situations will help you understand your lines better and develop your character more.

Delivering Dialogue

In this game, two players perform a dialogue in three different ways. Choose one of the four dialogues and get ready to develop your delivery.

Deliver your lines shaking hands.

Deliver your lines sitting back to back.

Deliver your lines staring in your partner's eyes.

Four Dialogues

Dialogue #1

PLAYER 1: You are a wonderful dancer.
PLAYER 2: Why, thank you.
PLAYER 1: Dancing tells a lot about people.
PLAYER 2: Really?

Dialogue #2

PLAYER 1: I didn't mean that.
PLAYER 2: What did you mean?
PLAYER 1: I don't know.
PLAYER 2: You don't know.

Dialogue #3

PLAYER 1: Sorry, I lost it.
PLAYER 2: How did you do that?
PLAYER 1: I didn't mean to.
PLAYER 2: I guess not.

Dialogue #4

PLAYER 1: So, you're new here.
PLAYER 2: Well, sort of.
PLAYER 1: I've never seen you before.
PLAYER 2: Never?

Developing Character

Does your character need more character? Choose one of the dialogues and try each of these ideas when delivering your lines.

Be Someone

- a thief and a police officer
- a witch and a wizard
- a king and queen

Be Somewhere

- an old graveyard
- a steep cliff
- a dark dungeon

Be Busy

- eat an apple
- wash the floor
- read a newspaper

Making Up a Play

First, you need an idea for a play. Think about conflicts and problems that upset you, about experiences and events that make you feel sad. Maybe something happened to you or to someone you know. It might be a story you heard on the news or that happened a long time ago.

Once you've got your idea, you need to turn your conflict or sad event into a plot. Start working with the most important things that happened in the beginning, middle and end of the conflict or event. Where does it take place? Who are the main characters? What do they do and say?

Before you start feeling overwhelmed by the job, try this improv game. Improvisation is a good way to develop plot, action, character and dialogue.

Serious Scenes

Here are four ideas for serious scenes to get your creative juices flowing. Give the actors a bit of time to think about what's important in the scene and how to play their roles. Then start improvising.

I Dare You!

Think about friends, rules and responsibility.

Roles: Group of neighborhood kids
Setting: Behind a shopping mall
Action: Hanging out after school
Rule: No graffiti on the walls
Conflict: One kid dares another to write her name on the wall.

Do It Now!

Think about childhood fears.

> **Roles:** Mother, father, child
> **Setting:** Dark basement
> **Action:** Parents rushing to get to work
> **Fear:** The child is terrified of the basement
> **Conflict:** Parents tell the child to get her bike from the basement, NOW!

Who's Guilty?

Think about guilt, innocence and what's not fair.

> **Roles:** Teacher, students
> **Setting:** Classroom
> **Action:** Writing a test
> **Guilt:** One student steals the answers and stuffs them into another student's desk.
> **Conflict:** The teacher accuses the innocent student of stealing.

Gang Up

Think about gangs, differences and bullying.

> **Roles:** New kid, gang, coach
> **Setting:** Basketball court
> **Action:** Shooting hoops
> **Differences:** The new kid doesn't understand English.
> **Conflict:** The gang bullies the new kid.

Shakespeare

Shakespeare wrote great comedies and tragedies, but he was also an accomplished actor. In the late 1500s and early 1600s, he performed in the famous Globe Theatre in London. It was here that audiences watched many of his plays. The original Globe Theatre burned to the ground in 1613 during a performance of Shakespeare's *King Henry VIII*.

The Globe Theatre

The original Globe Theatre looked a lot like a courtyard. There was no roof, so plays were performed only in warm weather. When a flag was raised from the tower, it meant that there was a show that day. The sound of a trumpet meant that the play was about to begin.

Poor Macbeth!

Shakespeare's *Macbeth* is the tragic tale of a brave Scottish general. As Macbeth is returning home after defending the kingdom, he meets a gruesome trio of witches brewing an evil spell. They tell him that he will soon be crowned King of Scotland. But how can that be? The king is well and has two sons to claim the throne.

Gradually, Macbeth's good nature is overwhelmed by ambition, and he decides to follow his wife's evil plot to murder the king. Step by step, Macbeth moves closer to his own destruction. He kills the king and everyone else who gets in his way. In the end, he dies on the battlefield at the hands of another loyal Scottish soldier.

Hey, Old Witch!

Shakepeare's *Macbeth* is full of witches, ghosts and bloody murders. This game will get you in the right mood to perform a scene from the play.

The players form a circle. One player stands in the center and starts to move like a witch. The group calls, "Hey, old witch, are you coming out tonight?" The witch replies in a very wicked voice, "No. I'm busy." The group asks, "Why? What are you doing?" The witch replies with something like, "I'm brewing a pot of poison!" Or "I'm dusting off my broom!" The group keeps asking the witch to come out, until the witch suddenly screeches "YES" and catches another player who then becomes the witch.

Macbeth: Act IV, scene i

Adapted by Deborah Dunleavy

Setting: A wild and windy heath in Scotland. Three witches sing and dance around a cauldron. They are preparing their evil potions.

(Thunder booms.)

FIRST WITCH: Thrice the brindled cat hath mewed.

SECOND WITCH: Thrice and once the hedge-pig whined.

THIRD WITCH: Harpier cries, "Tis time, 'tis time!"

ALL: Double, double, toil and trouble;
Fire burn and cauldron bubble.

FIRST WITCH: Round about the cauldron go;
In the poisoned entrails throw.

SECOND WITCH: Fillet of a fenny snake;
In the cauldron boil and bake.

THIRD WITCH: Scale of dragon, tongue of dog;
Eye of newt and toe of frog.

ALL: Double, double, toil and trouble;
Fire burn and cauldron bubble.
For a charm of powerful trouble,
Fire burn, boil and bubble.

178

(*The witches are startled. They stop dancing and look around.*)

SECOND WITCH: By the pricking of my thumbs;
Something wicked this way comes.

ALL: Open, locks, whoever knocks!

(*Enter Macbeth*)

MACBETH: How now, you secret hags of the haunting hour.
What is it that you do on this night so dark?

ALL: A deed without a name.

MACBETH: I must know what lies ahead.
If in telling me, the world should crumble,
Then let it be so. I must know. I must know.

FIRST WITCH: Speak.

SECOND WITCH: Demand.

THIRD WITCH: We'll answer. Or would you rather hear it from our spirit masters?

MACBETH: Call them. Let me see them, now.

IN THE WORDS OF SHAKESPEARE

Have you ever "laughed yourself into stitches," felt "tongue-tied" or "seen better days"? Have you ever "suspected foul play" because someone was "as dead as a doornail"? Did something just "melt into thin air"? Shakespeare made up all of these expressions.

ACT IV:
ON WITH THE SHOW!

Act IV takes you backstage where all the behind-the-scenes stuff is happening: directing, special effects, costumes, scenery, props and lighting. You might discover that your true talent lies in being a stage manager, a set designer or a director. Get ready to put on your very own play.

BEHIND THE SCENES

Have you ever watched a play and wondered who made the horse costume or who painted the castle? Take a peek behind the scenes and discover all the magical things that make a play come alive. There might be a job for you!

- Make a cardboard castle.
- Rummage through a props box.
- Advertise your play.

It Takes Teamwork!

It takes a lot of people doing a lot of work to put on a play. Mostly it takes a lot of teamwork. Remember: What goes on backstage can be just as exciting as what's happening on stage.

- The **director** tells the actors where, when and how to move on stage. Sometimes a director coaches the actors to help them get their characters just right.

- The **stage manager** is the director's number-one helper. This is a job for someone who is good at keeping everybody organized.

- The **properties person** collects, makes and organizes all the things — props — used by the players.

- The **lighting person** runs the lights for the show.

- The **sound-effects person** performs live sounds and plays recorded sounds.

- **Costume designers** and **wardrobe people** are in charge of creating the costumes, putting them together and keeping them clean and organized.

- The **makeup artist** helps the players put on their makeup and wigs.

- The **prompter** carries a script and is always ready to call out lines to players who might forget their parts.

- The **publicity person** is in charge of advertising the play and making sure the players have an audience.

- The **set designer** decides what scenery and props appear on stage. **Artists** and **builders** create the scenery.

The Stage

The kind of stage you see in most theaters is called a proscenium stage. It is useful to know how this kind of stage is divided. That way you'll know where to put the scenery and where to go when the director tells you to enter upstage left.

Upstage Right	Upstage Center	Upstage Left
Center Stage Right	Center Stage	Center Stage Left
Downstage Right	Downstage Center	Downstage Left

Audience

All the World's a Stage!

A play can be performed almost anywhere. Here are some places to scout out.

A Porch

Use the porch stairs for different stage levels. Enter and exit through the door. Seat the audience on three sides to give you an apron stage, just as in Shakespeare's time.

A Park

A park with gently sloping hills is like a Greek amphitheater. Stage the play at the bottom, and seat the audience on the surrounding hills. Slides and swings transform into anything from a jungle to a castle.

Sets and Scenery

In Shakespeare's time, a bush in a pot represented a forest, and a sign told the audience where the play was taking place. Not a bad idea!

Setting the Stage

A table and chairs can set all sorts of scenes, from a kitchen to a king's court.

Green and blue streamers and shiny fish hung from a basketball net create an underwater scene.

Transform boxes into a train or a fortress.

Backdrops

The scenery at the back of the stage is called the backdrop. Some backdrops are very detailed, especially when they have to set a mood on stage. Others are very basic; all they have to do is suggest a place.

Paint a scene on large sheets of paper and attach them to the back of the stage.

For a starry night, cut small holes in a piece of dark fabric, hang it at the back of the stage and shine a light behind it.

For a garden scene, hang old flowery curtains as a backdrop.

Flats

Flats are large, flat, rectangular pieces of a set that are joined together to make a backdrop.

Use cardboard flats attached to chairs to create different sets. Find six sheets of heavy cardboard, each 60 cm wide and 2 m high (2 ft. by 6 ft). Paint them different colors, or decorate them with swirly patterns or wallpaper. Use heavy electrical tape to attach a long piece of elastic to the back of each flat. Slip the elastic over the back of a chair.

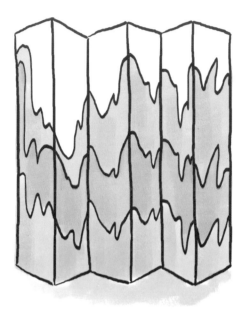

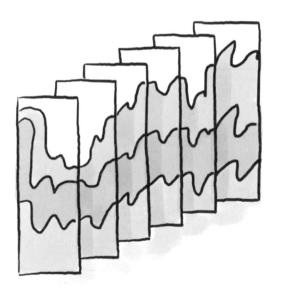

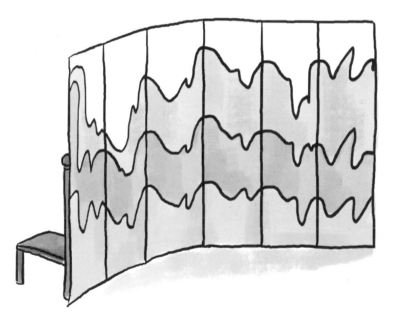

Four Scenes in One

You can make four different scenes for your play using two refrigerator boxes. Paint one scene on the two front panels. Turn each box to the left and paint a different scene. Keep turning the boxes until all four sides of each box match up.

Lights Up

It is important for the audience to be able to see the actors and action on stage at all times. Here are some things the lighting person needs to sort out.

Where?

An indoor scene usually needs a light coming from the top of the stage. Set the lights where the audience can't see them, and avoid shadows as much as possible.

How Bright?

Does the scene happen at night? Use table lamps for lighting. For an afternoon scene, try a low light coming through a window. A morning or desert scene needs intense light coming from the top of the stage.

When?

Some plays start with a blackout. The players enter, take their places and wait for the lights to come on. Sometimes the lights are on, and the players enter already in character.

Cone Reflector

A big square flashlight will brighten up a stage. Standing lamps and clip lamps also help. Make a floodlight by attaching a cone reflector to a clip lamp with a neck that bends. Ask an adult to help make your lights.

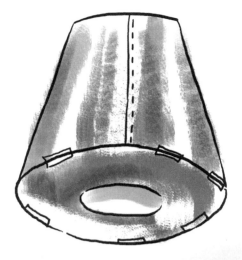

- Cover a piece of cardboard with aluminum foil, with the shiny side on the outside. Make sure all of the cardboard is carefully covered.
- Make a cone out of the foil-covered cardboard. Make the small end big enough to fit over the neck of the lamp. Staple and tape the cone.
- Unplug the lamp and take out the lightbulb. Place the cone over the neck of the lamp and tape it in place. Put the lightbulb back.

Colored Gels

Colored plastic sheets, called gels or gelatins, can be placed in front of the lights to create a mood. Most hobby or camera stores have gels. Make sure that the lightbulb does not touch the gel — the gel will melt. Here's how to make a gel frame.

- Use two pieces of cardboard that are big enough to fit over the end of a cone reflector. Cut a circle in the middle of each frame.
- Carefully cover the cardboard frame with aluminum foil, making sure the whole frame is covered.
- Place the gel between the two pieces of cardboard. Tape the cardboard together. Tape the gel frame to the end of the reflector cone.

Mix and Match

Put a blue gel frame over one light and a red gel frame over another light. When you shine the lights on the same spot, you get a purple light. What happens when you mix red and yellow lights?

Props

"Props" is short for "properties." These are all the things actors use in a play that aren't costumes or scenery. Start stuffing your prop box. Fill it with things that you might use in a play someday.

Costumes

Start a costume box right beside your prop box. Visit second-hand stores and rummage sales to pick up some wonderful things.

Tunics

With a simple tunic, you can become a pirate, a fairy, a prisoner, a scientist or a medieval fool. Just wear a T-shirt underneath or put a hat on your head. Decorate the tunic with beads, buttons and fabric paint.

You can make a tunic out of a big shirt. Cut off the sleeves at the shoulder and wrap a wide belt around your waist. You can also use an old sheet, tablecloth or piece of fabric. Cut a hole in the middle for your head, and you have an instant costume.

For broad shoulders, use a coat hanger.

Front of House

Let's go to the "front of house" and see what else needs to be done before opening night.

~~~~~~

Get the Word Out!

Now that you have a fabulous play, you need to let people know about it. Here are some tried-and-true ways to advertise and market your play.

Posters

Include some great art, the name of the play, where and when it will be performed and how much the tickets cost.

Press Release

Describe the play in a short paragraph. Mention where it will be performed and when, how much the tickets cost and where to buy them. Send the press release to your community newspaper and local radio and television stations.

Fliers

Make fliers and hand them out on street corners, outside a movie house or at other events. Dress up like a mime or a character in the play.

Opening Night

The audience arrives. The ticket-taker greets people at the door. An usher gives them a program and shows them to their seats.

Programs

Make enough programs so that everyone in the audience gets one. Put the name of the play and playwright on the front cover. List the scenes, characters and names of the actors inside. Thank the people who helped with the play and the performance, everyone from the director to the florist who donated the flowers.

> ## Merlin & King Arthur
>
> ### THE CAST
> **Merlin:** Josh Howard
> **King Arthur:** Abe Alexander
> **First Child:** Linda Stravinsky
> **Second Child:** Kate Pennazza
> **First Knight:** Willie Russell
> **Second Knight:** Susanna Reed
> **Third Knight:** Jasmine Fong
> **Sir Kay:** Jeffrey Yeates
> **Sir Ector:** Larry Polley
> **Onlooker:** Charlotte Alexander
>
> Thanks to: Chisamore Paints, Simpson's Hair Salon, M & R Costume Rentals and Mr. A. for the music.

Tickets

Make tickets out of strips of construction paper. Write the name of the play and the seat number on each ticket.

Places Everyone!

200

Glossary

Act (noun): a section of a play.

Amphitheater: a stage set lower than where the audience is seated.

Apron stage: also known as a "thrust stage." The audience sits on three sides.

Backdrop: scenery at the back of the stage.

Choreographer: a person who creates dances.

Comedy: a play or performance with lots of laughs and a happy ending.

Commedia dell'arte: Italian clowning and comedy dating back to the Middle Ages.

Dance drama: a kind of drama in which the movements of dance are used to tell a story.

Dance sack: a large bag made out of stretchy fabric. Players get inside the sack and move.

Dialogue: two or more players speaking to one another.

Domino mask: a mask that covers the eyes but not the mouth; also called a half-mask.

Farce: low comedy that is full of humor, slapstick and zany plots.

Flats: large, flat rectangular pieces of a set used for a backdrop.

Fractured fairy tale: a familiar story with a new twist.

Freeze: a position of freezing and holding a pose, as in a photograph.

Improvisation: a style of acting a scene spontaneously, without planning it beforehand.

Melodrama: a kind of drama with exaggerated emotions and stereotyped characters.

Mime: a kind of drama in which players use their bodies to express emotions and act out a story.

Monologue: the speech of one player saying his or her thoughts aloud to another character or to the audience.

Narration: the part of the script that describes details that aren't part of the action.

Narrator: the person who speaks or reads the script's narration.

Neutral: a way of posing or standing without any expression or movement.

Neutral mask: a plastic mask with no expression.

Pace (tempo): how fast or slow a player moves, acts or speaks.

Pitch: how high or low a sound is.

Plot: the action or events in a play.

Proscenium stage: a stage that has the audience seated in front of it.

Projection: "throwing" your voice so that everyone in the audience can hear.

Readers' theater (RT): a kind of drama in which players read words from a story or script; no sets, costumes or scenery.

Scene: a short section of a play.

Slapstick: comedy full of physical humor.

Story theater: a kind of drama in which players read the words from a story or script and use sets, costumes and scenery.

Stress: the emphasis on a word or in a sentence.

Tableau: a scene in which a group of players holds a frozen pose to tell a story.

Tempo (pace): how fast or slow a player moves, acts or speaks.

Theater of the mind: a term to describe radio plays.

Tragedy: a play with a sad story.

Volume: how loud or quiet a sound is.

White-face: a style of makeup used by mime artists to create a neutral expression.

Index